Art in Your Visual Environment

SECOND EDITION

Gerald F. Brommer
George F. Horn

Davis Publications, Inc.
Worcester, Massachusetts

Art in Your Visual Environment

SECOND EDITION

Graphic Design: Penny Darras-Maxwell
Cover illustration: Diane Nelson

Printed in the United States of America

Library of Congress Catalog Card Number: 84-73494

ISBN: 0-87192-169-3

AYVE—2ND. ED.

10 9 8 7 6 5 4 3 2

Contents

How to Use This Book

Art in Your Visual Environment is a resource book that can be adapted to suit many teaching styles and types of curricula. There is abundant material here. Teachers and students should be stimulated by the book's many ideas, concepts and techniques, and should feel free to begin reading anywhere. Any or all of the sections will help students become more aware of the importance of art in their environment.

Several important areas of art are emphasized: careers in art; how art affects our environment; the elements and principles of art; the history of art; the interpretation of art as a means of communication; and the making of art. Any or all of these can be studied in depth or can be used as motivation for creating art itself. Teachers are encouraged to base their program schedules on personal needs and available time. No two classrooms will use this book in the same way.

Many museums and contemporary artists have shared their work with us so that we can learn from their excellent examples. Teachers and students have also generously provided us with a wide range of expression. These are not examples to be copied, but should serve as sources of information as we explore styles, subject matter and concepts. Our own expression is most important and valuable, and the book is designed to encourage awareness, creativity and sound judgment.

Art in Your Environment is just what the title says it is—a collection of examples from around the world that makes us aware of the importance of art, both in our daily lives, and as a means of sharing and expressing our ideas.

The Importance of Art in Your Life

1 The Visual Impact of Your Environment

The Visual Variety Around You

Your environment—the world around you—is much more than a tall tree, an attractive house, a network of roads or a dazzling fountain in the city square. True, these may be parts of the world in which you live, but a close study of your environment reveals many other elements. Biological and physical things affect the way you live and the quality of your life. Social, political and economic elements help form your attitudes and guide your actions. Aesthetic elements around you can give you a sense of pride, joy and delight in your daily life.

A general definition of environment, then, includes everything that is. The *natural environment* is land, air, water and living things. The *human-made environment* is the product of people. People use the natural environment to build and make the things that we all use and enjoy. These parts of the environment do not exist by themselves. They depend upon each other.

The natural environment is not only wide views of the central plains or a scenic coastal area. It is also our local parks and paths, flowers, leaves and other natural details.

Many of us live in the human-made environment of our nation's cities. That environment (in all its forms) constantly influences our senses, perceptions and visual awareness.

We encounter parts of both natural and human-made environments every day, on our way to school and home again. Can you see how the environments work together in this scene?

Furniture, graphics, record covers, electrical equipment and floor coverings are part of our human-made environment.

An old house in town might be your favorite because you like its form, textures, color, details, history or surroundings. Add it to your sketchbook.

The many things around you affect your developing perceptions. These visual elements include your home, community and school; shopping malls, signs, television commercials; labels, street lights, sidewalks, motor bikes and the countless other components of your daily life.

How do you react to the many different things that you see each day? Is there an automobile, a poster, an old house or a great oak tree that has a special appeal to you? Do you know why this might be?

As you pursue your study of art and do art on your own, it might be helpful to do several of the following:

1. Carry a sketchbook and sketch those things that interest you.
2. Redesign a favorite cereal package.
3. Make a clay model of a neighborhood pet.
4. Redesign an automobile or motor bike.
5. Make a crayon rubbing of tree bark, a crack in the cement sidewalk, or a piece of rough-grained wood.

These and other art activities help make you visually aware. They help you look more carefully at the environment around you. Looking carefully is very important to people who make art.

As you study art, you will become more aware of textures, forms, values, contrasts and colors that surround you.

Artists often make us more aware of the environment. Colleen Browning painted Clyde's Car. Through the painting, she draws our attention to graffiti, people, city travel and the New York environment. (Kennedy Galleries, Inc., New York). Christo wraps parts of our environment to draw our attention to its forms and characteristics. Wrapped Coast in Australia was covered with a million square feet of plastic.

Creative architects use common materials in unusual ways. The IBM building in Boca Raton, Florida, was carefully designed by Marcel Breuer Associates so that sections can be added when they are needed. Such additions will not change the basic architectural plan or make the building less attractive.

Understanding Architecture

Architecture is public art. Any building, large or small, has some visual effect on people who pass it. Some buildings may attract people, while others may be rather ordinary. Yet all are there for the public to view, and are important parts of our visual environment.

Buildings such as houses and apartments are designed to be lived in. Although there are many ways to lay out rooms, all these contain similar basic living spaces: kitchens, dining rooms, bedrooms and bathrooms.

In contrast, other kinds of architectural structures in your community have been designed for special purposes. Office buildings are designed for local businesses, factories are built for making products, and public and private buildings are made for education, museum collections, theater productions and sports events. There are also churches, synagogues, stores and transportation terminals.

As you can see, buildings are shaped by their uses. A finished building must contain space that is useful to people who live or work there. Both the space inside a building and the space outside are important.

As architects and planners redesign the center of Pittsburgh, they construct new buildings and remodel existing structures. The towering United States Steel Corporation building (designed by Harrison & Abramovitz) and Three Rivers Stadium (above) are examples of architecture built for a special purpose. Can you see plans for transportation?

Condominiums and apartments are designed to house many families in a single structure. What kinds of problems may this cause for architects and builders?

A stadium, for example, provides space for events such as baseball, football or concerts. There must be enough space for people to perform comfortably. There must also be enough space for people watching. There should be bathrooms, food stands, ticket booths and so on. Other architectural concerns are parking lots, entrances and exits of the building.

What the building looks like is just as important as what is inside. After the steel, glass, brick, stone and mortar have been put together into a solid, practical structure, the building will be seen for many years. An architectural design can be beautiful or ugly, and it stays that way for a long time. Once the structure is finished, it is hard to take away.

An architect is a very important person. He or she decides how buildings will look, outside and inside. Architects discuss the purpose of the structure with the owner, and then design the space to be enclosed. They plan the interior layout, keeping in mind where the building will be and what it will be made of. The architect may also use this information to estimate the cost of construction.

Interior spaces should be designed to be beautiful and practical. Thousands of people must be able to move easily through the Renaissance Center in Detroit. There must be casual seating, shopping and eating areas and plenty of exits. The building must be visually stimulating inside and out.

Architectural design is a commitment. The exterior of the L.B.J. Library at the University of Texas at Austin is simple and direct in form and use of materials. It is visually attractive.

Architectural teams use computers to find out how much their building materials will cost, and how much material they will need. The computer stores many details about construction. New equipment and techniques constantly change how architecture is planned.

Architectural designs usually start from *floor plans* that show how the building will be laid out. *Elevations* show where windows and doors will be, and what they will look like. *Architectural renderings* show what the building will look like from the outside, and what the area around it will look like. Finally, a three-dimensional *scale model* of the building is made. It looks like the finished building, but is very small. After the building's design is approved, workers dig the foundation on which the building is built.

Examine buildings in your community, such as office buildings, stores, the local stadium. Are they successful architectural forms? Do you like to look at them? Do you think the exterior (outside) designs show what the buildings are used for? Do the exterior designs seem to match the inside of the buildings? Do the buildings relate to other nearby buildings or landscapes? How do you feel about the

Architectural renderings (below) and models (above) show clients how their finished buildings will look. Many media and techniques are used for these presentations. Blueprints and floorplans give builders measurements and directions for construction.

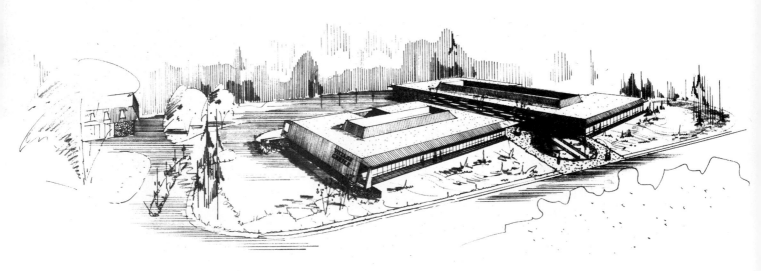

After office space has been planned, designers draw the arrangement of walls, furniture, traffic flow, storage and reception spaces. Such drawings help interior designers select colors, materials, lighting, office furniture and floor coverings.

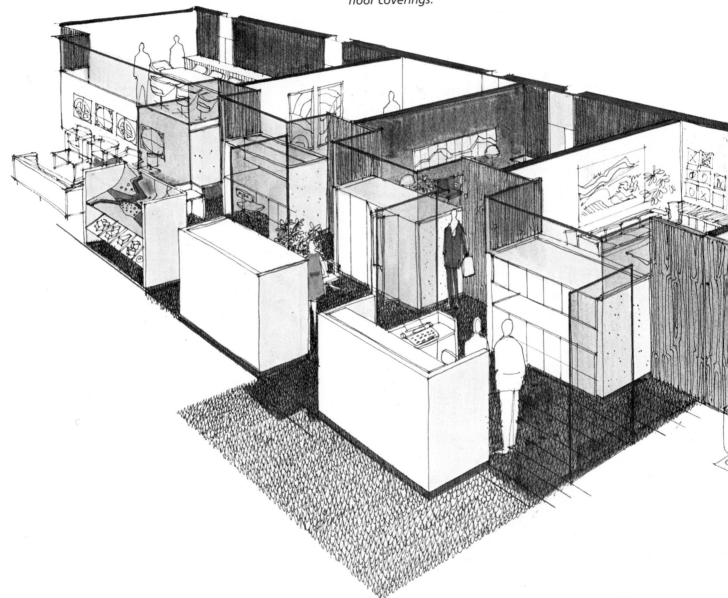

Environmental designers should consider form, color, texture, size and architectural style as they develop plans for city centers. Downtown Houston is seen in this photograph.

An important part of urban renewal is the preservation of buildings that link the present with the past. In this picture, the dome of the historic City Hall in Baltimore is being repaired.

materials these buildings are made of ? Which building do you like the best? Why?

Now think of the architecture in your community as if it is all related. Think of each building as a part of a total environment. Buildings, open spaces and areas of trees and flowers must be placed carefully. People can create beautiful spaces after studying an area and talking to the people who live there. When people plan carefully, old buildings can be fixed, buses and subways can be improved and an entire neighborhood can be made to look better. This type of planning is the work of environmental planners.

Recently, people who want to improve cities have talked with government groups, city planners and ar-

chitects. Together they have started projects for cities. These projects should keep cities from decaying.

A good master plan is needed, not only for bringing older cities back to life, but also for creating new cities. Such plans usually affect all parts of the urban environment: buildings, transportation, where people walk, business and industry.

This drawing shows the master plan for a new community outside of Philadelphia. Echelon will have commercial, business, residential and educational areas connected by a large transportation system. Open spaces and landscaped areas are planned, as well as routes to interstate highways, turnpikes and rapid transit lines.

When making a master plan, an architect or planner must look at more than a single architectural structure. He or she must also look at how buildings affect each other, and how they affect people. When a planner looks at a whole area, he or she must plan open spaces, fountains, sculptures, benches and trash containers. More and more designers of downtown areas understand that people who spend time there each day like to look at beautiful things. In many places, there are strict laws about signs: they cannot be larger than a certain size, they cannot use neon, they cannot hang over the street. These laws may make cities more beautiful.

People try to keep cities from decaying because they want to create a more pleasing environment for human activity. Successful projects have given many cities a new life. When a city is pleasant to live and work in, more businesses move there, and more people care about how the city looks.

What do you think of how your community looks? Are there parts that you feel are interesting, orderly and beautiful? Do you find some parts messy and ugly? Call or write to local government agencies, planners and architects who may be working on renewal projects. Find more about what is being planned for your city.

An enclosed pedestrian area (above) links two high-rise buildings in downtown Houston. Enclosed and open pedestrian areas allow people to move about more freely in crowded spaces. Architectural details, such as this light standard (right) add interest to streets, plazas and malls.

The center of Portland, Oregon, combined reconstruction, remodeling, new construction, dramatic plazas and environmental planning to produce a unified architectural space. It is the center of other mall redevelopments. The area was planned to create a sense of beauty and order.

Architects sometimes plan how cities or buildings might look in twenty years or more. This architectural drawing shows the city of Houston with a transportation system built into a pedestrian level.

You may enjoy building a model of an office building, home, church (above) or an urban renewal project (left) as these two students have done. The model at left shows a street for traffic, a pedestrian bridge, a circular park with a waterfall, several buildings, benches and trees.

Suggested Activities

Here are several activities to guide you as you study architecture in your community.

1. Make a map of your neighborhood including houses, stores, streets and other important features. Use this information to develop a plan that you feel will make the neighborhood look better.
2. Design a small park or playground for a lot that is not being used in your neighborhood. Let a fountain or sculpture be the main point of interest in your park.
3. Redesign the exterior sign of a shop in your community. Think about what is sold or done in the shop. Think about how the shop fits into the surrounding area.
4. Design a poster based on a theme such as: "Work for a Better Environment," "Pollution is a Mess" or "Clean up Your Neighborhood."
5. Redesign a room in your house. When you make the floor plan, think about the purpose of the room. How big is it? Where are the doors, windows and closets? Perhaps you can build a model and design furniture for it.

Notice the many messages that can be seen from this single street corner. There are messages from local and national companies. Notice how the graphic designer of the Kodak–Magic Mountain billboard used empty space, a simple message and a powerful illustration to dominate the scene.

The Influence of Graphic Design

Advertising and graphic design are multi-billion dollar businesses. We are all influenced by graphic design and advertising. Every day you see many symbols and images designed to tell you to buy products and services. If advertising were against the law, how would manufacturers tell us about their products?

What do graphic design and advertising art include? The range is very broad: posters on buses and in store windows; billboards; three-dimensional displays in stores; packages and labels in the supermarket; booklets and pamphlets of all types.

You can find examples of graphic design in your home, too. Newspaper and magazine ads and colorful pictures in books are examples of graphic design. When you watch television you see many moving, multicolored images designed to promote products. Record album covers are also examples of graphic design. Have you ever bought a record because you liked its cover?

This newspaper advertisement is the result of several graphic designers working together: a fashion illustrator (Stephen Bieck); an art director, who designed the layout; a typographer for type selection and typesetting; and layout and mechanical artists for the production work. Notice the design of the advertisement. The message is presented in a logical sequence: illustration of fashion items, product name (NEW DIRECTIONS), store name (Robinson's), prices and phone number in boldface type and finally the detailed information.

Robinson's
NEW DIRECTIONS

You'll find all the components you're looking for this season in New Directions, our men's department that represents the state-of-the-art in sportswear. From the trendy to the traditional. The European to the American. The fun to the serious. But always the newest, at prices that will let you take in both dinner and the show.

At left: Our own Shetland wool/acrylic crewneck sweater in apple green, orchid, wheat, strawberry, canary yellow, fire red, sky blue, burgundy or navy. S-M-L-XL. **$26.** With belted polyester/cotton twill slacks in taupe, sand or black, sizes 29-34. By Generra™ **$25.**

At right: Cotton corduroy blazer in sand, taupe or grey. 38-44 regular, **$40.** Sweater vest in plum and olive jacquard shetland wool. S-M-L. **$35.** Button-down oxford cloth shirt in new deeper tones of blue, putty, mauve or salmon cotton/polyester. S-M-L. **$20.** Stone-washed indigo cotton denim jeans (for an authentic faded effect) in sizes 28-34, we added the belt, **$28-$30.** All by Generra™ in Robinson's New Directions, 99/145, all stores except Palm Springs. To order, call toll-free **1-800-523-7600.**

CHALLENGE: Abstract thoughts.

Portraying the passing of time, youth, and dreams.

How to communicate or symbolize an abstract word or thought challenges all artists. How do you *show* "time" or "youth" or "dreams?" We challenged photographer Jason Hailey to illustrate all three. So he created this symbolic composition incorporating a child, a "castle of dreams," and the proverbial shifting sands and tides of time. To capture a wide tonal range, and the texture and detail of both the sea and the sand, he chose Kodak Ektachrome 64 professional film (daylight). He used a Hasselblad camera with a 50 mm lens, natural light with reflector fill, and varied exposures and f stops to provide a selection of results. For more information, write Eastman Kodak Company, Dept. 412L-134, Rochester, NY 14650.

Solve your photographic challenges with Kodak products.

The photography of Jason Hailey is featured in this Kodak advertisement. The illustration first draws our attention. The word "challenge" stands out next. We wonder what "challenge" has to do with the photo. The Kodak logo is seen next, and then the explanation of the challenge.

Graphic designers work in many media to present their messages and ideas. They use any art material that will make their work attractive and different from the work of others.

Often, many graphic artists work together. A design studio might do a promotional brochure, for example. To do the brochure, they need photographers, type artists, writers, illustrators and layout artists. There are many different parts of a brochure. Each part must fit together with the others to make a good graphic design.

Most advertising design includes two main elements: illustration (pictures) and lettering. The illustration makes you look at the advertisement. The lettering tells you about the illustration. The illustration can be drawn, painted, photographed or done in mixed media. It can be brightly or subtly colored or in black and white. It can look real or sketchy, like a cartoon or like a photograph.

There are many styles of lettering. There are alphabets in all type styles. These styles can be old-looking, or very modern, thick or thin, with serifs (cross pieces at the ends of letters) or without. Many type styles can now be created on computers. Graphic artists must select the type that is right for each job.

Computer graphics artists can use an almost-endless number of type styles and variations. This Genigraphics slide (including color, type and special effects) was made on a General Electric computer.

Advertising illustrator Roger Hagen used wash drawing to portray a display cabinet. A graphic designer then combined various sizes of lettering with the illustration to compose this newspaper advertisement. Notice how the type attracts attention and then informs.

College students in a package design class learn to plan and design boxes, bottles, packages and labels. These students may now be designing the things you see on store shelves. Art Center College of Design, Pasadena.

Bottles, boxes, containers and labels are planned by graphic designers. Look at the different items in your supermarket. Good design is needed to successfully market products.

Designing labels and packages is very like designing posters and signs. Labels have more writing (copy) on them than posters because labels must list what is inside a package and what the product is made of. But label design must be as powerful as poster design. In fact, the visual force of a label must be so strong that it attracts your attention and asks you to take it from the shelf.

Packages are made to hold certain things. Some are made of plastic. Others are made of cardboard, paper or glass. Some are bottles, while others are boxes, cans or cartons. Some packages and labels give you an idea of what is inside. Think of the many cereal boxes in your grocery store. Each box holds a similar product, yet they are different shapes, sizes and colors. Some make you look at them; others do not.

You can tell when a label is well designed. You can find it easily on the shelf. If you use a product again and again, soon you spot it because of its unique design. You don't even look at its name.

Some designers work in three dimensions (length, width, depth) instead of on flat surfaces. You can see their displays in store windows and shopping malls. There is not much to read in these displays. Most displays are made of interesting shapes and forms. They look a little like exhibits. Visit a shopping center to see how many types of displays you find. Take photographs or make sketches of those you like best.

Displays such as this one are seen in many types of stores. The display designer needs to understand package design, display techniques and poster design to make this single sales aid.

The pages of magazines and books begin with sketches such as this one. Here the graphic designer balanced type and illustration to emphasize the illustrations.

Graphic designers (or graphic artists) work with type and illustrations. Editorial graphic artists use type and illustrations to design magazines, books and brochures. They use the same elements advertising designers use, but for different purposes. Advertising designers help sell products or ideas. Graphic artists work on books and magazines to create attractive pages that people will want to read.

In graphic design, artists work together. They see themselves as part of a team. An art director is in charge, but each artist carries out one part of the assignment.

Look at art magazines and books, travel folders and other published materials. Study the pages to see how the type and illustrations are arranged. Good layouts are simple and organized. All graphic designers must understand and use the same elements and principles of design that you will study in Chapter Three.

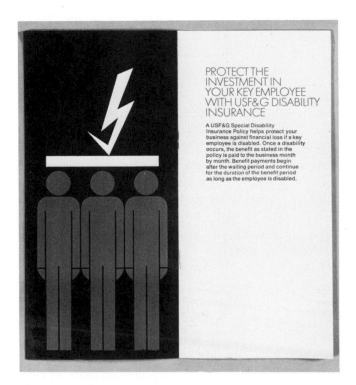

PROTECT THE
INVESTMENT IN
YOUR KEY EMPLOYEE
WITH USF&G DISABILITY
INSURANCE

A USF&G Special Disability
Insurance Policy helps protect your
business against financial loss if a key
employee is disabled. Once a disability
occurs, the benefit as stated in the
policy is paid to the business month
by month. Benefit payments begin
after the waiting period and continue
for the duration of the benefit period
as long as the employee is disabled.

Note the simple design, the large amount of white space and the contrasting right and left pages of this folder.

The desk of book designer Janis Capone shows some of the steps in designing a book cover. At the upper left is a comprehensive layout, with type pasted in and illustration spaces blocked in. Photographs are at center top, with sizing and cropping directions. The printed, full-color cover is at lower center, with the finished books at the right.

GIRL SCOUTS

Saul Bass and Associates designed the new logo for the Girl Scouts of America. Above is the old symbol; below the new logo. Note how the overall shape is the same while the concept is new. How does this graphic symbol better represent the organization? Discuss its symbolism.

Here are four logos that immediately identify products or services nationwide. One uses a word, while the others rely on visual imagery to identify the companies.

When you see a logo (General Electric's, for example, or McDonald's) and you know what company it belongs to, you are recognizing the work of graphic designers. Logos are used to identify companies and their products, buildings and stationery.

Some logos are designed around company initials or names: AT&T, GE, Coca-Cola, VW and Ford are some of those. Other logos are designed around symbols such as Chrysler's star, McDonald's golden arches, CBS's eye, American Telephone and Telegraph's bell in a circle. Cut some logos with symbols and some with initials from magazines or newspapers. Design the layout for a double page display of them.

Why are logos important to companies? Are visual symbols easier to remember than words? Why may this be so? Why is it important to recognize things? Why are graphic designers important in the world of business?

Can you find the logo of Davis Publications on the cover of this book? Why is this logo meaningful?

Architects design structures that are pleasing to look at and to live in. Graphic designers create graphics that help you identify such buildings. Graphic designers also create signs that are attractive and useful.

Signs that are well designed help people who do not speak our language. During the Olympic Games, for example, people from many countries had to find out where things were. Signs and symbols told them simply, no matter what language they spoke. Why must people understand signs? Where else must signs be understood by people of many languages?

Photograph or sketch architectural graphics in your community. Are there some that you like? Should some be made more attractive or more modern?

Visual symbols are combined with numbers and type to provide directions on this unique signpost. Why are symbols often used more than words?

This example of architectural graphics combines an attractive logo and lettering in a simple and effective sign.

Study these package designs. Can you redesign any to make them more attractive? The photographs of Alice S. Hall are used on many record jackets. Can you redesign a record jacket using a magazine photograph, travel poster or one of your paintings as the visual image? The size can be smaller than a real record, but it should be square. Cut out or paint the type.

King Printing Company

Suggested Activities

1. Look around. Become familiar with the world of graphic design. Notice words in a poster, on a package or on a sign. How do they fit together? How many type sizes and styles are used? How is color used? Why are some words larger? What are the differences between illustrations in a clothing advertisement and those in a poster or a package design? Choose a poster, a package or a newspaper ad. Redesign it, or several. Use the elements and principles of design discussed in Chapter Three in this book. Plan your design. Make small sketches first. Complete the design in actual size.

2. Is your school presenting a play? Is the school telling you the importance of health or safety? Design a poster that announces or promotes either activity.

3. Do you have a favorite record? What kind of illustration or symbols go with this record? Design an album cover. Remember that it should include the name of the song, the name of the group and the illustration.

4. What makes your town or city different from other towns or cities? Design a sign that tells travelers about one thing that makes your community different. The illustration must attract attention. Try not to use too many words. Your city council may be interested in your design.

Cross Keys Inn

Ryland Homes

Why are these three logos effective and appropriate for their companies? Can you design logos for several companies in your community?

This student poster might give you an idea for a poster for your own town. Stick-down type, available in art stores, was used for the lettering here.

35

2 Careers in Art

There are many different careers in the field of art. You can see the creative work of career artists almost everywhere, from the museum to the supermarket.

However, you may not have thought about the many ways that artists and designers shape your life. Their visual ideas add color and interest to your daily activities.

Look at your own home. The shape and appearance of the furniture, appliances, lighting, draperies, wall and floor coverings were all determined by designers. Your clothes and jewelry are also created by artists and designers. Artists create illustrations in books, magazines and newspapers, packages and containers for products, comic strips and political cartoons. Television scenery, costumes and even commercials are designed by artists. Your house was planned by an architect. Cars are designed by stylists. What other things around your home are designed by artists?

Make a list of things in your community that artists may have planned or created. Look for posters, billboards, signs and displays in your town. There might be interesting sculptures in a shopping mall or in front of a new building, or a mural on a large wall.

Years ago, young people were employed by art studios as apprentices. They learned specific art skills

The work of artists is all around us. An architect, interior designer, lighting designer and retail display designer were involved in making this department store interior attractive and functional.

Fashion design students are getting expert advice from a professional designer. Such experiences help student designers understand the working world of art.

and gradually became skilled enough to start their own studios or shops. Today, college or art school training helps students relate their talents and interests to specific career areas. On the following pages, you will learn about some art careers. The competition for these careers is great, jut as it is in many other fields. But if art is important to you, think about a career in art for your future.

You are now enrolled in an art class. As you go through this text, be aware of the techniques and media that interest you. You will feel more comfortable working with some media than with others. This may give you direction for choosing a career in art.

Interior designers work with furniture, wall and floor coverings, fabrics, color, art, light and natural plants to create a comfortable interior. This one was developed by Steve Chase and Associates for a home in Palm Springs.

Environmental Planning and Development

If you look around you, the work of environmental planners is easy to see. Buildings are planned, designed and built under the direction of architects. Other artists design the spaces in and around the buildings.

Buildings begin with the concepts and sketches of architects. Then architectural delineators paint or draw their ideas. Drafters finish the plans and blueprints. Contractors finish the construction. Other artists, such as interior designers, space planners and landscape architects design, build and decorate the interior of the building.

Large buildings need teams of artists to complete their design. These artists are either employed by the architectural firm or are free-lance designers. Free-lance designers work for many different architects.

Architects not only design high rise buildings but also plan our houses, apartments, churches, temples, schools and shopping places.

Interior designers not only decorate interior spaces, they may actually design furniture, wall coverings and lighting fixtures. They plan colors, fabrics and accessories to fit people's needs. Some interior designers specialize in department store interiors. Others work with offices or homes.

Landscape architects design the environments around buildings, plan walkways, seating areas, lawns, trees and planting areas. They contour land and design drainage and watering systems.

All art careers related to environmental planning and development require study in colleges or art schools. People interested in these careers should be good at drawing, three-dimensional projects and painting. They should like to work on projects with other people.

Architect Marcel Breuer used prefabricated units and large open spaces to design these IBM offices in Boca Raton.

There are many special career areas in architecture. Here, a model builder finishes a scale model.

Commercial Art and Design

Art careers in the commercial world are often in the areas of television, publishing, theater and interior design. Commercial design, however, includes the areas of *graphic design, industrial design* and *fashion design.*

Graphic designers can go into many specialized fields of work. But all graphic designers work with the elements of illustrations and text (pictures and words). The illustrations may be painted, drawn or photographed. They are used to attract customers or viewers. The words (or type) are designed to communicate the message. Graphic designs include posters, billboards, advertisements, packages and record covers. The use of electronic equipment (computers,

Fashion designer Lynn Cartwright works on a swimsuit design for Catalina. Some of her designs were also used for the 1984 USA Olympic Team.

This graphic designer is trying out a label idea for a small can. His comprehensive design includes color, size, design and type. It will be sent to the printer for production.

40

laser scanners, photocopiers) is becoming an important skill in many large graphic design studios.

Industrial designers work with three-dimensional form. They design the products we use every day. These products include telephones, ball-point pens, automobiles, lightbulbs and furniture. Industrial designers work with metals, glass, plastics and wood. They are concerned with how well their products look and work.

Fashion designers design our clothes. But it takes many skilled people to complete the cycle from fashion idea to finished product.

Artists working in the many areas of commercial art and design must draw well, have a good sense of color and know how to use the elements and principles of design. Industrial designers must work well with three-dimensional objects and sculpture. They must also work well with many materials and tools. College or art school training is necessary for a successful career in these highly-competitive areas.

This design for a possible Ford automobile is the product of several industrial designers. It is actually a clay model, spray painted and detailed to look like a real car. The model is made to test customers' reactions.

A graphic designer gives several pieces of art to a television art director. The art director then combines the images on a TV control panel. Any combination of images can be made and sent out to the public.

Entertainment and the Media

We live in a media-oriented society. Films, television, books, magazines and theater events entertain and educate us in many ways. Television, film and publishing companies employ many artists to design and finish their products.

Art careers in film and television include sketchers, special effects people, animators and electronic graphics programmers. Many artists design cartoons for television and film. When you watch the flashy electronic effects in television commercials, you are watching graphic art that requires a specially-trained designer. Costumes also need to be planned and made; sets designed, built and painted.

Many art careers are also related to theater and stage production. Costume designers, set and scenic designers, lighting directors and makeup artists are needed for stage plays, operas, ballets and puppet performances.

Gil DiCicco is working on a background panel for an animated film. Painted characters will perform in front of this scene.

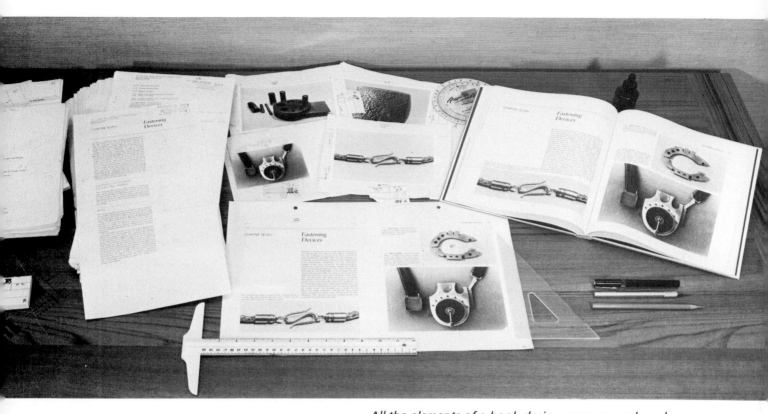

All the elements of a book design are arranged on designer Janis Capone's work table: the text typeset on galleys at left; the illustrations in the upper center; the two-page mechanical (pasteup) at lower center; and the finished book at right.

Books and magazines allow authors to communicate ideas. But illustrators, book designers, layout artists, cartoonists and other artists are needed to produce the pages of those books and magazines. There are dozens of art careers associated with publishing. Think of all the catalogs, advertisements and brochures that come in the mail. Greeting cards and comic strips also need artists to think of ideas, design the illustrations and lay out the pages.

Photography is an essential part of any art career in media. Photographers may specialize in photojournalism (news), fashion, foods, products, sports, illustration (for books and magazines), advertising or architecture. Some photographers work in medicine, law or the fine arts.

Careers in entertainment or the media are often quite technical. They often require study in colleges or art schools. Drawing and design skills are needed in most art careers. Some also require skill in using technical equipment.

Cultural Growth and Enrichment

The careers we have discussed so far are practical applications of art—designing and selling products and ideas. But there are other artists who work by themselves and make products for others to enjoy. Some artists make paintings, sculpture or jewelry. Some teach art. Others work in museums or galleries.

The careers of fine artists differ from other careers in that the artists are self-directed. They make their paintings, photographs, prints and sculptures to suit themselves. They hope someone will like their work enough to buy it.

Craftspeople work in the same way. They produce ceramics, jewelry, textiles, weavings, glass, etc. to sell to galleries or at shows.

It is often difficult to earn a living by sellling paintings or jewelry. Many fine artists and craftspeople earn extra money by teaching. People who wish to become art teachers need special training in art education.

All kinds of art, from all ages, is displayed for us to enjoy and study at museums. Many art careers are related to museum work.

Most art is sold in galleries. Gallery directors, owners and staff assemble art and craft work, arrange displays and organize shows. The gallery is an agent for fine artists and craftspeople. It displays and sells their art to the public.

There are also careers that combine art and writing. Articles about art and artists appear in art magazines and newspapers. Writers often visit galleries and museums to review shows or interview artists and directors.

These art careers require much schooling and training. Artists and craftspeople must learn techniques and skills before they can create excellent work. Teachers, writers and museum personnel must also learn their skills.

Teachers must be skilled in many techniques to help people learn about arts and crafts. Teachers need to enjoy sharing their knowledge.

Restorers who work for museums are skilled artists. They work on valuable pieces of art and must be very careful. This artist is retouching a drawing that is several hundred years old. The artist is working in the restoration laboratory of the Los Angeles County Museum of Art.

David Freda is a metalsmith. He is working on an elaborate jewelry piece that he designed. Fine artists and craftspeople must enjoy working alone and setting their own production schedules.

Bill Robles is a court and police artist. He sketches people in places where cameras are not allowed, such as law courts. His work is often shown on television news.

Services By and For Artists

Some art service careers use artists' talents (police and court artists, restorers of paintings); some deal with artists and their work (art materials dealers, framers, shippers and photographers of art); and some relate to the business of artists (lawyers, accountants, agents, show coordinators). Some of these careers are only related to art, and the people involved need not be artists themselves.

Some art service careers are built around combinations of interests (education, psychology and therapy, for example). Others combine a strong interest in art with expertise in another field (art history and library science).

Many service careers demonstrate the creative thinking of ambitious people. For example, a person may enjoy working with a television camera and go to art collectors' homes to videotape collections for insurance and/or inventory control.

Summary

These few pages provide only an overview of art-related careers. If you are interested in an art career, learn as much as you can about all types of art and take as many art courses as possible. Your high school art teacher and guidance counselor will be able to give you more advice and help you learn which colleges or art schools offer the best programs.

You should be aware that there are many careers in art. All of them require drawing skills as well as an understanding of different techniques and materials.

Frederick Hammersley's oil painting is titled Sacred and Pro Fame *and is 45" × 45" (114 × 114 cm).*

3 Looking into Art: How Is It Constructed?

You can see design in all parts of your world: your home, playground, school and neighborhood. Everything in your visual environment can be described in terms of *line, shape, form, space, color, value* and *texture.* These qualities are called the *elements of design.* They exist in your environment and in your art.

Look closely at your environment. Look at the many *lines* created by branches of a tree and the symmetrical *shape* of a leaf. Look at the rounded *form* of a rock; the *space* between houses; the bright or soft *color* of flowers; the contrasting *values* of light and dark in the sun on a warm summer day. Look at the *textures* of brick, wood and glass.

If you sketch things around you, you will become more aware of the elements of design.

Artists use the elements of design in many different ways. All artists create their art according to several basic concepts, however. These concepts give artwork order. They are known as the *principles of design.* They include *balance, unity, contrast, pattern, emphasis, movement* and *rhythm.* You can see these principles in your environment. Look for *balanced* rocks; *unified* colors in a landscape; *contrasting* values of light and shadow. You can see

patterns of waves at the shore; the *emphasis* of bright flowers on desert cactus; visual *movement* as you look along a path. You can sense the *rhythm* of days and seasons.

As you work with art materials and complete the art activities suggested in this book, you will become more aware of the importance of the elements and principles of design. As you begin to understand them better, you will find you have more satisfaction and success in making art.

The Elements of Design

The elements of design work together. Two or more can always be found together in natural things, in things we make and in art. Look at a tree leaf. The leaf has *shape* and *color.* The veins of the leaf form a pattern of *lines.* What elements of design can you see from where you are now sitting? Look around and make a few notes or sketches.

Before you can make the elements of design work together in your art, you must understand each one. As you work on art projects, you may want to reread this section on the elements and principles of design. They will help you plan and create your art.

Study Robert Vickrey's egg tempera painting, Landing Circle, and see how artists use the elements of design. Notice lines *between the paving stones, in the chalked circle and in the painted white stripe.* Shapes *include the paving stones and planes.* Find form *in the three-dimensional quality of the artist's daughter.* Space *is created by painting planes and paving stones smaller as they recede.* Colors *are subtle and controlled.* Look for values *in the light and shadows on the girl.* Visual textures *appear on pavement, cloth, hair and wood.*

Robert Vickrey also used the principles of design to organize the elements in this painting. He achieved balance *by placing the girl in the upper right and the cluster of planes at lower left.* Notice unity *in the color and texture of the painting's surface.* Contrast *can be seen in many places: light and dark; hardness and softness; human and mechanical.* Pattern *appears in the pavement's repeated shapes and lines.* Emphasis *is placed on the figure.* Visual movement *is felt as your eyes are led from plane to plane and then to the isolated figure.* Rhythm *is provided by the repeated pavement shapes and the irregular positions of the planes.*

All the elements and principles of design work together in this painting to produce a unified work.

49

Lines that are thick and thin create a feeling of three dimensions. These were not drawn. They were cut freehand from black construction paper.

Soft wire is a three-dimensional line. You can form it by hand to create linear sculptures. What other materials can you use to create three-dimensional line art?

Line

What is line? Where do you see line? How many different kinds of line do you see in your home? In your neighborhood? List examples of line that you see on your way to school and inside your school. During the course of this study, you will look for three kinds of lines.

First, there are many illustrations of *actual line.* Look at magazine and newspaper drawings, for example. Look at drawings of clothing, furniture and machines. Look at cartoons. These lines are used to show you people, objects and ideas.

Second, there are lines that are not really there. They are called *implied lines.* You can find implied lines on the edges of buildings, objects and other three-dimensional forms. If you draw the outline of a person, the line that you draw on a piece of paper may create a shape. The shape might look like the person. But the person is not linear at all.

A third type of line is a *three-dimensional line.* What does this mean? Can you think of examples? A chain-link fence makes a pattern of lines. But the wire the fence is made of is three-dimensional: it has length, width, and depth. Yet because it is thin it looks like a line. Trees, flagpoles and overhead wires are all three-dimensional lines.

Other kinds of lines are also important. Vertical (up and down) lines give you the feeling that you are moving up. Horizontal (side to side) lines are restful and calm. Diagonal lines (lines that go from the lower corner to the upper corner) are active and moving. What is your feeling about a curved line or an S-shaped line?

Are all lines smooth and unbroken? Look for fuzzy lines, broken lines, lines of dots. How is a black line on white paper different from a white line on black paper? Have you seen the lines painted down the

Felt marker pens in several colors and widths were used to make this simple, attractive line drawing. What other subjects would work well with this technique?

White and black wax crayons make these lines on gray construction paper. There are three values in the art, but the lines are dominant.

middle of streets? Some are white. Others are yellow. They may be unbroken or broken. Why is this? Why are they painted white or yellow?

Line Activities

Take a 3' length of soft wire (stove pipe, aluminum or copper) and make a three-dimensional line sculpture of an active animal or person.

The illustrations on these pages may help you start on your own line activities.

Make lines with a variety of materials: pencil, crayon, chalk, pen and ink, brush and paint. Can you make a line design with needle, thread and a piece of cloth? Roll out a flat slab of clay and create a line drawing or a line pattern on its surface. Do the materials you use affect the kind of line you can make? How?

Shape and Form

Move a marker across and around a piece of paper, starting near the edge. Make a single line that ends exactly where you started it. You have just enclosed space with a line. You have created a shape. You may have created a geometric shape or a free-flowing shape. You may even have made a shape that is the outline of a person, animal or object.

Now experiment with a piece of clay. Model it into a ball, a cube or something else that you like.

These two activities show you the difference between shape and form. *Shape* is flat and two-dimensional. *Form* is three-dimensional.

You can find many examples of shape and form around you. Have you noticed shapes of color in draperies, wallpaper, tiles, rugs and clothes? Did you ever think of lamp bases, appliances, furniture, pillows or an old football as forms?

Geometric shapes and *forms* have sharp, clear edges. The square, the triangle and the circle are geometric shapes. The cube, the pyramid and the sphere are geometric forms. In both old and new architecture, architects often use geometric shapes and forms. Do you think architects use geometric forms and shapes because they make buildings look orderly and organized?

Bert Wasserman used straight lines and color to produce this painting. It emphasizes geometric shapes. Hard and clean edges are needed to make this kind of painting successful.

A student used ink to outline leaf shapes and a vase. The added newspaper emphasizes the organic shapes. The solid background is a single negative shape. It focuses attention on the positive shapes of leaves and vase.

There are many examples in nature of *organic shapes* and *forms.* They are free-flowing and irregular. Clouds are soft, changing organic forms. Are people and animals geometric or organic forms?

Look for examples of geometric and organic shapes and forms in your environment. Look for them in the work of artists, architects and designers. How does an artist use shape to show an idea? If an artist uses color or texture in a shape, does it make the shape look different? Do some shapes seem to show movement or direction?

Shape and Form Activities

Use a ruler and pencil to make ten lines on a sheet of paper. The lines should cross each other. Use tempera to paint the shapes you create with lines.

Look at the examples on these pages and create your own shape or form activities.

Use clay to make three-dimensional forms: a ball, box, animal or person.

What forms can you make with scraps of wood? With pieces of cardboard or paper? With cloth scraps?

Harrison McIntosh used a potter's wheel to produce the two ceramic forms seen here. He attached them to a chromed metal base. This creates a contemporary ceramic sculpture that emphasizes dramatic geometric forms. Louis Newman Gallery, Beverly Hills.

The clay figure, made by a student, is a good example of three-dimensional organic form. What other subjects are examples of three-dimensional forms?

53

Architects focus on interior and exterior space. John C. Portman, designer of the Renaissance Center in Detroit, provided spaces for movement, rest, viewing, seclusion, dining and meeting.

In her bronze sculpture Oval Form, *Barbara Hepworth interests us in the overall form and the rhythms of interior voids. Franklin J. Murphy Sculpture Garden, UCLA.*

Space

Space is all around you. You may think, then, that *space* is everywhere. Sometimes there is very little space around you. There is little space in a telephone booth or a small car. But have you ever stood in the middle of a large empty school auditorium? Or alone on the fifty-yard line of a football field? Or looking out over the wide, open space of a desert or a big farm? How are these places different from one another? How are they the same?

The world is an environment that moves in unlimited space. When you fly in an airplane and move through just a small part of this space, you may be surprised and almost afraid.

The element of space is important to the work of the artist, the designer and the craftsperson. The sculptor creates realistic or abstract forms that take up space. Many sculptures of today have open space (voids) in their designs. The architect designs buildings that enclose space. A school building is often a huge form. Its large amount of space is divided into smaller spaces for classrooms, halls and offices. How do painters, graphic designers and craftspeople use space in their work?

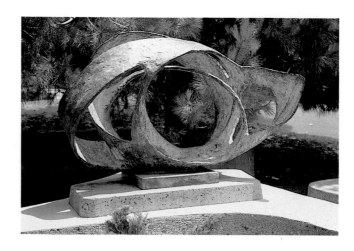

Like the other elements of design, space is an important feature of your everyday world. Space can be as small as a small box or as big as the endless universe. Think about and write down the different spaces that you move through or see each day.

Space Activities

Look at the section on drawing and perspective in chapter 4. Look at the space. Try some of these ways yourself in a small pencil drawing.

Letter your name in several ways. Try to make the letters look as if they move *into* the picture plane.

Collect photos from magazines that show: interior space, deep space, shallow space, crowded and empty space and movement in space.

Arthur Secunda used flat colored paper to express a feeling of great space. In his collage, Distant Islands, *color intensity changes to imply distance.*

The graphic illustrator who made this drawing wanted to show depth and space. How was this accomplished?

Janet Fish is a master at painting glass, reflections and light. In Stack of Plates, *1980*, she emphasizes color and its effect on glass. She had to look very closely to see all the subtle changes in hue and value. Can you find the primary and secondary colors in the work? How has she used value to show light? Robert Miller Gallery, New York.

Chuck Close divided a large sheet of paper into small squares. He used a conte crayon to fill the squares with different values of one color. How could he make dark, medium and light values with a single color? Squint your eyes or stand back from the page to see a more realistic image. Can you use this pencil technique to draw a still life, a basketball or a self-portrait? Pace Gallery, New York.

Color, Value and Texture

Perhaps the most stimulating things that you see and notice are color, value and texture. These words describe how objects look on the outside. Color, value and texture are called surface qualities. You may select a particular shirt or dress to wear because of its pattern of bright reds, purples and oranges. People often say a rainy, cloudy day is a gray day because what you see is a range of dull, monotonous values. Have you touched things that gave you a pleasant feeling because of their surfaces? Or gave you an unpleasant feeling because they were rough, coarse or prickly?

Think hard about color in your home and community. See how many different colors you can discover. How many have you looked at but never noticed? You will find out that green is not just green: there is a broad range of greens. Some will be light; others dark. You will come across some colors that are bright and intense, and others that are dull.

Color has three basic properties: hue, value and chroma. *Hue* is the name of the color. *Value* is the lightness or darkness of a color. *Chroma* means the intensity of brightness or dullness.

Use colored pencils or watercolors to illustrate some of the things that you see. Try to match the colors in a single object, such as a flower. Limit your colors to primary hues: red, yellow, blue and black. You will have to mix these colors to make others. What colors combine to make green? Orange? Violet? How can you make a green darker?

Look at things around you that are made of wood, concrete, brick or metal. Rub your hand across the side of a shingled house, the trunk of a tree or the back of your cat or dog. How would you describe the textures? Place a plain piece of paper over a crack in the sidewalk. Rub a crayon over the paper. What happens? Do the same thing with paper on a wood plank. The different effects that you experience by touching or rubbing are the result of variations in *texture.*

Color, Value and Texture Activities

Design a color wheel that shows primary, secondary and intermediate hues. Use your own design.

Emphasize value in a painting, by using a single color. Add black and white to produce a variety of values.

Use typing paper and black crayon to make rubbings of fifteen different textures. Use these in a collage or design a texture display.

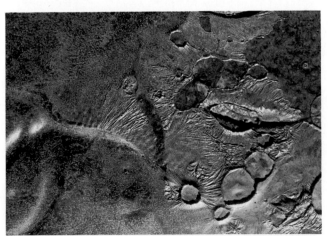

Textures can be actual or simulated (made to look like textures). Otto Natzler (left) used tools to make actual textures in the side of a ceramic pot. The textures in the student work (top) were made by placing the paper on different three-dimensional textures and rubbing with crayon. This picks up the surface qualities.

Principles of Design

Balance, unity, contrast, pattern, emphasis, movement and rhythm are the principles of design. You can see examples of them in your natural and human-made surroundings. Tree limbs are large near the central trunk, but the outer branches are smaller. Together the branches create a pattern and seem to move outward and upward. The same tree can also have a sense of balance and unity. On your next trip from home to school list things that are good examples of each principle of design.

You will want to show organization and order in your artwork. Do contrasting colors or related colors make your idea work best? How much movement and rhythm should you design into a clay model? How can you create an interesting pattern in a block print? Study the illustrations on these pages. Become familiar with the various principles of design. They should become a natural part of your thinking as you develop your own skills in using the many different kinds of art materials.

Balance

What is meant by balance? How does balance affect you? How do you react to the different kinds of balance found in a natural object, a building or a piece of art?

When you stand still, with your feet together and your body straight, you are in a position of static balance. If you move your body forward or backward, you will soon have to shift your feet or keep yourself from falling. Your body will be unbalanced at that moment.

In a way this illustrates two of the three kinds of balance that you will discover not only in your environment but in artists' work. These two kinds of balance are called formal or symmetrical balance and in-

Jerome Kirk's sculpture is designed to move with air currents. Its appearance is constantly changing. But it is always in informal balance. Why?

formal or asymmetrical balance. A third kind is called radial balance.

In a design based on *formal balance,* all the objects or shapes are arranged on an imaginary vertical central line. Stand straight with arms at your sides before a mirror. Think of a line running down the center of your body. Note that everything to the right of the line is basically the same as that on the left. This is one illustration of formal balance. Can you think of others?

In contrast, a design based on *informal balance* may have a large shape located on one side of a central vertical line. The large shape may be balanced by a smaller shape, farther away on the other side. Now as you stand in front of the mirror, shift your hips as far as you can to one side. To keep your balance, your head and shoulders will move in the opposite direction. Study your reflection. The images on one side of the center line are quite different from the

Look at these three works of art. What kind of balance did the artists use? Analyze each and discuss the compositions. A student made the batik design. Audrey Flack painted the self-portrait in oil (Courtesy Louis Meisel Gallery, New York). Judy Chicago painted Through the Flower *using acrylic paint and an airbrush.*

images on the other side. Your body now shows informal balance.

Radial balance is the third type of balance. It creates a feeling of radiating or spinning from a central point. A familiar example of radial balance is a wheel, with its spokes moving out from hub to rim. Flowers and the sun also show radial balance.

Balance Activities

Make a mobile using wire, thread and cardboard shapes. Emphasize informal balance.

Make a model teeter-totter (see-saw) and use it to show both symmetrical and asymmetrical balance.

Look through magazines and collect two pictures each of formal, informal and radial balance. Make a display for your bulletin board.

Make two masks (or drawn clown faces), one showing formal balance and the other showing informal balance.

Contrast

You can see a good example of *contrast* when you compare day and night. Stand at the front door of your house and look out on a sunny day. Note how clearly defined everything is. If you stand at the same spot on a dark night, what changes can you describe? Why?

Look for contrasts, particularly in the area between your home and school. Keep a list of contrasting sizes, shapes and colors of plants and animals. Sketch some of these.

There are many interesting contrasts in your human-made environment. Are the buildings in your community the same size, style or color? What contrasts can you see even within a single building? Did you think of contrasts in what the building is made of—glass, brick, stone, metal or wood?

As you study works of art, you will find many contrasts. There are contrasts in style—abstract or realistic. There are contrasts in size—small figures or huge environmental sculpture. There are contrasts in color—brightly-colored designs or softly-colored ones. You will also see how artists use different kinds of contrast for certain effects. Strong, contrasting colors, textures and patterns in a design are dynamic. They give the design a sense of activity. Softer colors and textures seem still and give a sense of quiet.

Contrast Activities

Use your camera to take pictures of contrasts that you find at school or home.

Make a clay animal and give its surface smooth areas and textured areas.

Make a black and white drawing. Emphasize the contrast between dark and light values. Make your drawing dramatic.

Many materials were used in this student work (watercolor, collage, pencil, pen and ink). Notice the contrasts: textured and smooth areas; dark and light; organic and inorganic shapes; patterned and nonpatterned areas. Can you find more contrasts?

Unity

What is unity? Why is the principle of unity important to the artist-designer? Do you think of words such as "singleness," "oneness," and "completeness" when you think of unity?

When the artist-designer creates a design (painting, poster, automobile, wall hanging), it often has many small parts. For example, a painting of a city may include automobiles, buildings, streets, signs and trees. A true test of *unity* is how well these parts go together. If the parts of a painting do not hold together, it does not have unity.

Look at plants, leaves, seed pods and other natural forms. Look at a shopping mall or an office building. Study the artwork in a local exhibit or at the museum. Do you see how these things show unity? Can you think of things that show *dis*unity in your physical environment or in a work of art?

Unity Activities

Make a clay pinchpot. Use a single tool to create a unifying surface pattern.

Create a small mosaic design using small squares of colored paper. Using squares of the same size gives a feeling of unity.

Use similar brush strokes, pencil lines or pen and ink lines to create a painting or drawing that has a unified surface.

The consistently hard edges and flat shapes create a unified feeling in Owh! In San Paõ, *an oil painting by Stuart Davis. What other features establish unity? Whitney Museum of American Art, New York.*

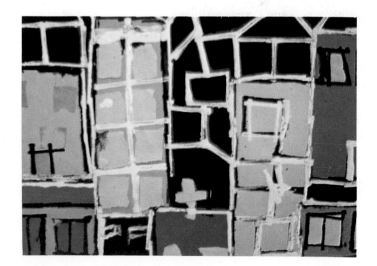

This student painting achieves strong unity through the pattern of lines that define the buildings.

61

This crayon scratchboard design is filled with many patterns. There is an overall pattern effect with no area of emphasis. The folk-art quality creates a charming design.

A student artist used criss-crossing lines to produce shapes. These were painted to create an irregular pattern. Does this give you an idea for a painting project?

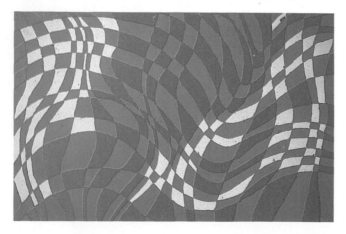

Pattern

People often think of pattern as surface decoration. A pattern is etched into the outer surface of a ceramic bowl; the threads and yarns in a wall hanging make a pattern; a zebra's stripes form a pattern. Look for examples of pattern around you. You will find there is a wide range. Rather free, random arrangements of objects can form a pattern. Patterns can also be made of units, or motifs, repeated over a surface at regular intervals.

Pattern makes things look richer and more exciting. The artist and designer know this, and use many patterns in their designs. The architect, for example, creates different patterns in a building. These patterns can be made by brick, stone, doorways and windows.

Where do you see pattern around you? Just about everywhere. In the supermarket, packages on the shelves make one kind of pattern. Clouds make patterns in a blue sky.

Pattern Activities

Cut many of the same shape from colored papers. Arrange them on paper of another color to make a repeated pattern.

Carve shapes, initials or designs in linoleum, plaster or clay. Print the shape again and again on paper.

Photograph patterns you see on buildings, material, blankets or clothing. Arrange a display of your photographs.

Emphasis

As you look at things around you, certain parts stand out, while others remain in the background. Bright colors seem to come toward you; dull colors seem to fade. Large forms are easier to see than smaller forms. This play of contrasts adds interest to your visual world. If there were no emphases the world would be boring. It would all seem the same.

The artist uses different degrees of *emphasis* in a painting or a sculpture. This is done so that your eye will move through the design in an orderly way, from one point to another.

The graphic designer may give emphasis to an important word on a poster by making it larger than others. An architect can make the main entrance of an office building stand out by changing the area around the building and choosing special building materials. The tower or steeple with a cross on top emphasizes the religious nature of a church or cathedral.

Look for emphasis in your natural and human-made environment. Where do you find emphasis in natural forms such as trees and flowers? How do

Arthur Secunda made the various colored papers by hand. He then tore them into rounded shapes and created this abstract collage (above left). Where is the center of interest? How did he emphasize it? What contrasts can you find?

The graphic designer who planned this attractive architectural sign (above) was very careful to emphasize EMERGENCY. Why is this a good idea? In what ways did the designer achieve emphasis?

artists use line, shape, color, value and texture to create emphasis in a painting, a print, a piece of sculpture or a hand-crafted necklace?

Emphasis Activities

Collect ten cartons, labels or advertisements. Make a display of them. Discuss how you used emphasis in your display to show names or products clearly.

Collect ten or more illustrations or photographs from magazines. Decide what part of each illustration is emphasized. Where is the center of interest? Circle it with a marker. Discuss how the picture creates movement to bring your eyes to the center of interest. What did the artist or photographer do to create movement in these areas?

63

One of Titian's paintings is the basis for this study of movement. A student used watercolor and ink to emphasize only the movement found in the original painting. Can you follow the movement in the study?

Movement and Rhythm

Movement and rhythm are important qualities of life. Think about the steady changes from day to night and the regular sequence of the seasons. They produce a kind of movement and rhythm that make life interesting.

Artists use movement and rhythm to breathe life into their designs. Have you noticed how artists repeat shapes, colors and values? How they repeat textures in different parts of a sculpture or in crafts objects? Have you seen how the architect creates patterns of windows in the sides of a building?

The artist-designer arranges shapes, colors and textures so that your eye moves in a certain direction—*movement*—throughout the design. The *rhythmic* qualities of the design may range from smooth and flowing to exciting and tense.

Some artists develop rhythmic movement in three-dimensional form. Alexander Calder, a famous twentieth-century American artist, invented the mobile. A mobile is a moving, rhythmic form that constantly changes as air moves it.

What things in your visual environment have movement and rhythm? Study the artworks in a local exhibit at your school or museum. Look for the kinds of movement or rhythm they show.

Movement and Rhythm Activities

Listen to several kinds of music. Try to draw the rhythm of each kind of music with line or shape.

Study some famous paintings. Think about how the artists lead you to the center of interest.

Use crayon on tracing paper to trace only the *movement* lines from several paintings. Or project a slide on large paper and draw the lines that show movement.

Alexander Calder's mobile, Pomegranate, *moves with the air currents. The repeated shapes produce visual rhythm, even in a still photograph. Where is the center of interest? What kind of balance does the artist use? Whitney Museum of American Art, New York.*

Summary

The elements of design are line, color, value, shape, form, space and texture. All artists work with these elements to create their art. These words are the vocabulary of visual artists—the raw materials from which art is made.

The principles of design are balance, unity, contrast, emphasis, pattern, movement and rhythm. They tell us how to use the elements. They help us show ideas. They are the grammar of visual artists— they help us to use the vocabulary of art (elements).

The elements and principles of design are used together. They work best when we combine them, because they help each other.

Study the small collage below. How many elements of design has the artist used?

Which kind of balance is used? How is the work unified? What contrasts can you find? Where is the emphasis? How has the artist created the center of interest? Can you find pattern? The movement and rhythm are strong and direct us to the center of interest. How are movement and rhythm emphasized?

Ask these questions about several other works of art in this book. Ask similar questions about your own work as you plan your art.

Wood scraps of similar sizes establish rhythm. Color emphasizes the forms, and creates more rhythms. The scraps' vertical and diagonal positions move your eye up and out. Can you feel this directional movement?

4 The History of Art: Foundation for Understanding

Who carved the first sculpture? Who designed the first building or painted the first wall decoration? We do not know who these artists were, of course, but they started a chain of action that continues today.

The first major art form was architecture. Pyramids, temples and fortresses were very important. But later, decorations in the form of paintings and sculptures became part of the buildings. There was a unity of the arts.

At certain times in history, architecture was the principle art form. At other times, painting, technology or concept interested artists the most. However, all types and forms of art are always created, no matter which style or method is the most popular at the time.

European and then American art was influenced by the Roman, Greek and Egyptian cultures. Different styles and concepts of art were developed at the same time in Asia and Africa. These Asian and African artists were sometimes more sophisticated and better craftspeople than the Europeans. The work shown here is from ancient times. It shows the fine talents and abilities of artists from different parts of the world.

The earliest art is found in caves in different parts of Africa and Europe. But, the earliest cities, civilizations and their art developed in China, India, Mesopotamia, Southeast Asia, Egypt and the Middle East (about 5000 B.C.).

This Sumerian stone sculpture is from Mesopotamia (2600 B.C.). It has a relaxed stylization and large eyes, which the Sumerians considered "windows to the soul." Los Angeles County Museum of Art.

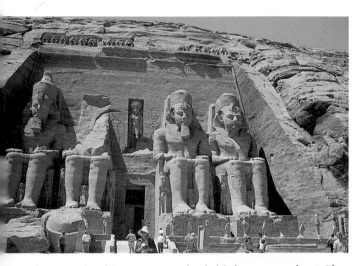

The Egyptian king Ramses II had this huge temple at Abu Simbel carved from a solid rock cliff. The king himself was depicted four times in the work, which dates from 1257 B.C.

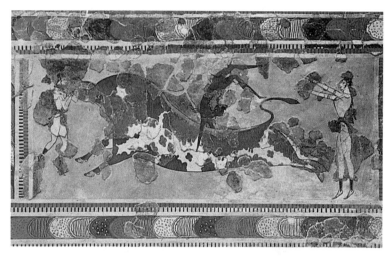

This colorful fresco (painting on plaster) is from Knossos (approximately 1500 B.C.). It shows athletes vaulting over a charging bull. Archaeological Museum, Candia, Crete.

Egyptian Art

The pyramids of Egypt were built about 2500 B.C.). They are still standing after more than 4500 years. These huge structures were built as tombs for Egypt's kings. Other types of tombs were also built, such as the sculpted temple of Ramses II at Abu Simbel.

North of Egypt, on the island of Crete, the Minoan civilization developed a city complex at Knossos (about 1600 B.C.). They built a three-story palace, known for its corridors, rooms, plumbing and advanced planning. It also contained marvelous sculptures and paintings.

Ancient Chinese artists mastered the techniques of bronze casting. This covered ting (from 500 B.C.) shows exquisite skill and craftsmanship. Los Angeles County Museum of Art.

The Parthenon, finished in 432 B.C., has become the artistic symbol of Greece. It is seen as the ultimate example of classic architectural beauty and proportion. It shares the Acropolis (high point) in Athens with several other fine temples.

The Colosseum could hold fifty thousand people. It is probably the grandest Roman structure. Underground corridors, seating areas and many passageways provided easy access for the public.

Greek, Roman and Early Christian Art

In 447 B.C., Greek architects and sculptors designed the Acropolis in Athens, crowning it with the beautiful Parthenon. This temple for the goddess Athena was built according to strict mathematical formulas. It is considered classic in its proportions. The Greeks used columns to hold up roofs. They sculpted in bronze and marble and decorated with mosaics and paintings.

Greek architects built theaters into their hillsides, and designed marketplaces for business and harbors for their sea-going trade.

The Romans copied many Greek ideas in painting and sculpture. But architecture was the greatest Roman art. Romans used arches to span rivers and built aqueducts that brought water to their cities. Huge structures were built to house many people. Roman architects were the first in history to design large interior spaces.

Romans also invented the dome to cover larger open areas and concrete, to help construct huge buildings and walls. They designed basilicas for court sessions and Roman baths like today's large gymnasium/fieldhouses. Roman forums were the city meeting places and markets. They painted frescos, designed mosaics and continued the sculptural traditions of the Greeks.

When the Roman Emperor Constantine became a Christian, his followers moved their churches from underground caves to buildings. They used the basilicas for church services, adapting that type of construction for their religious purposes. Early Christian artists decorated these interiors with mosaics and frescos that told Biblical stories.

The basilica of St. Apollinare in Classe (in Ravenna) was finished in 549 A.D. It is built according to the plans of most other basilicas: long, narrow, with side aisles and a rounded apse for the altar. Notice the original mosaics on the side walls and in the apse.

This marble sculpture is a Roman copy of an original Greek bronze, done by the artist Myron. The Discus Thrower *is life-size. It was originally cast about 450 B.C.*

The Hagia Sophia (finished in 537) set the style for Byzantine architecture. Its huge interior was covered with glass mosaics that illustrated Bible stories. The minarets were added by conquering Moslems in 1453.

Tilman Riemenschneider carved St. Burchard of Wurzburg from lindenwood in about 1500. It is 31" (81 cm). This skillful artist also carved huge altarpieces that have many detailed figures. He created them for Germany's Gothic churches. National Gallery, Washington, D.C.

Byzantine, Romanesque and Gothic Art

In 330, Constantine moved his capitol to Byzantium. He changed its name to Constantinople (now Istanbul). The new empire lasted a thousand years. It was at its peak in the sixth century. Byzantine art is known for its glass mosaics, painted icons and churches built on the Greek cross plan of four equal arms. The crowning architectural effort was the construction of the Hagia Sophia (Church of the Holy Wisdom). Its huge dome was 104 feet in diameter and was supported by four huge piers (groups of columns). The interior height of 141 feet was the largest interior space in the world, at that time.

During the Middle Ages (about 400–1000 A.D.), European art was made by monks. They copied Biblical material and illustrated the manuscripts with elaborate calligraphy, intricate designs and miniature paintings. The cultures of China, Japan, India and Mexico also produced wonderful works of art and architecture at that time.

Giotto painted his Madonna and Child *as part of a larger altarpiece for a church in Florence, Italy, in 1330. It is 34" (86 cm) tall, and tempera on a wood panel. The gold background and the halos are part of an older Byzantine artistic tradition. National Gallery, Washington,* D.C.

The Gothic cathedral in Cologne is Germany's largest. It was finished in 1332. Its carved stone towers dominate the city's modern skyline. Compare its size with the surrounding buildings.

During the Romanesque period (about 900–1150), European artisans worked on large stone cathedrals. The church became the major patron of the arts. Religious themes and buildings were suggested and paid for by church leaders. Barrel vaults and thick walls provided large interior spaces for worship. Sculpture was restricted to small areas around the main doors, and expression was emphasized in the carved figures. Small stained glass windows were introduced, but the interiors were dark. Romanesque art relied on Roman and Byzantine art but also looked at folk art for direction.

While Romanesque art was primarily rural, Gothic art (about 1150–1400) was the art of the developing cities. Merchants and tradespeople erected monuments of stone and glass to their god. Pointed arches, flying buttresses, huge stained glass windows and abundant sculpture were characteristic of Gothic art. These huge churches took many many years to build. But, because all the architects and artists involved had a single goal—to glorify God—the buildings are amazingly unified.

The Gothic art and architecture of northern Europe (see the Cologne cathedral) differed from that of Italy. The Byzantine tradition remained strongly influential in Italy. Painting became a very important art form. Giotto was the leading artist.

Renaissance Art

While architecture was the main art form during the Gothic period, painting and sculpture highlighted Renaissance art. The Renaissance (which means "new birth") began in central Italy and spread throughout Europe. Its artists and writers wanted to revive the classical concepts of Greece and Rome and emphasize the importance of humans and their environment.

Early Renaissance painters tried to make their subjects look real and solid, not symbolic. Gradually, everyday subjects and ancient mythology appeared in their work. It became important to show the richness of fabrics and metals.

The Italian Renaissance was supported by the wealth of the Church and its popes. They hired the best artists (Michelangelo, Raphael and Bramante) to make Rome the art capitol of the world. In Northern Italy, Titian and Giorgione worked with color and value to produce convincingly realistic paintings. Their paintings illustrated contemporary, mythological and Biblical themes. Leonardo da Vinci was as interested in the sciences as in art. Da Vinci was a true Renaissance man.

In Northern Europe, the Renaissance began in Flanders. Artists such as Jan van Eyck and Peter Brueghel painted in extreme detail. Both religious and contemporary themes were popular. German artists (Albrecht Dürer and Hans Holbein, for example) followed the Flemish tendency to paint small with great detail, rather than the Italian's simple yet large style.

Some artists in Southern Europe developed personal styles that exaggerated shapes and colors. They were called Mannerists. El Greco in Spain and Tintoretto in Italy were the most important of these artists.

Baroque art continued into the seventeenth and eighteenth centuries. It was led by Bernini and Caravaggio in Italy. Leaders in Northern Europe were Rub-

Michelangelo sculpted The Pietà *in 1500, using a single block of marble. Notice his careful attention to anatomical accuracy, and his ability to make stone look like fabrics. St. Peters, Vatican City.*

ens in Flanders and Rembrandt in Holland. Baroque artists drew, sculpted and painted realistically with great ease and skill. They pushed even further, however. They began to emphasize the drama and power of their subjects by using swirling forms and dramatic lighting. It was generally an expressionistic art. But, a few, like Vermeer in Holland, painted quiet interior scenes, and emphasized the qualities of materials and light.

Artists in France, England and America also began to make important contributions to the world of art. They often emphasized the fancy and the frivolous.

Giorgione used tones of color to create a three-dimensional feeling in Adoration of the Shepherds *(1505). He carefully observed the light, and emphasized space in the environment. Notice how the figures sometimes blend into the background. National Gallery of Art, Washington,* D.C.

Rembrandt made many self-portraits. This one from 1636 shows him at the age of thirty. The golden colors, deep shadows and emphasis on the face are typical of his Baroque style. Norton Simon Inc. Foundation, Los Angeles.

Jan Vermeer painted Officer and Laughing Girl *in about 1660. The Dutch artist emphasized the natural light coming in at the window, lighting the figures and interior space. Frick Collection, New York.*

Nineteenth Century Art

The nineteenth century in France saw the frivolity of late Baroque art (called Rococo) come to an abrupt halt with the severe Neo-classic style. Jacque-Louis David, Jean-Auguste-Dominique Ingres and Elizabeth Vigée-Lebrun painted in the classical styles and themes of Greece and Rome. The solid, simple, hard-edged forms in their paintings seem sculptural. At the same time, architects designed buildings to imitate ancient columned structures.

Modern art began with Neo-classicism. Academies were opened to study the form and content of art, both past and present. However, the government-endorsed Neo-classicism was not for everyone. Artists

Francisco Goya's The Second of May *is 110″ × 132″ (273 × 342 cm). It was based on an incident that the artist remembered from several years earlier. Notice the violent action, Oriental overtones, nationalist theme and heroic subject. These and the huge size are typical of romantic painting in the nineteenth century. Prado Museum, Madrid.*

Elizabeth Vigée-Lebrun painted portraits of Europe's well-known rulers (such as Therese, Countess Kinsky, 1793). This Neo-classic painting shows the countess dressed in a style that reflected ancient Roman tastes. Norton Simon Inc. Foundation, Los Angeles.

Gustave Courbet was one of the earliest French Realists. His Still Life: Apples, Pears and Primroses on a Table (1871) shows a still life exactly as it was. It has no hidden meanings. It simply shows us what the artist saw. Norton Simon Inc. Foundation, Los Angeles.

Thomas Eakins, an American Realist, painted The Gross Clinic as a commission from the medical students. It was so realistically done that some people fainted when they first saw it. The 95" × 78" (244 × 198 cm) work is done in oil. Jefferson Medical College, Philadelphia.

who could not tolerate restrictions, expressed their feelings with Romantic ideals and passions. They looked back to the Middle Ages (Crusades, historic wars, explorations, Oriental travels) for pictorial ideas. The drama of nature (storms, avalanches, floods, huge vistas) attracted their interest. These artists illustrated the works of Romantic writers and visualized ideas from the Bible. Delacroix, and Gericault in France, Turner and Constable in England and Goya in Spain became well known.

Artists who were not comfortable with either Neo-classicism or Romanticism, created a natural and cool realism in their artwork. Courbet showed ordinary men, women and objects in everyday situations (walking, cooking meals, fishing, going to funerals). European and American Realists showed real objects, colors, and people. Subjects were observed with great care and were painted that way. Artists did not interpret, idealize or romanticize their work. Such realism was the basis for Impressionism.

For the first time, artists had a choice of directions. They could select a style that best suited their personal needs for expression.

Notice the soft edges and dappled light in Auguste Renoir's Moulin de la Galette. *These are typical of his Impressionist style. The happy subject and active figures appear almost as a snapshot. The 1876 oil painting is 51″ × 69″ (131 × 175 cm). The Louvre, Paris.*

Some Impressionist artists worked in several media. The Little Dancer Aged 14 *is a bronze sculpture by Edgar Degas. He is best known for his paintings and pastels of ballet dancers. He also painted and sculpted horseracing subjects. Tate Gallery, London.*

Impressionism and Post-Impressionism

French artists became the leaders in developing the style of Impressionism. Painters moved outdoors to record their reactions to light, color and movement. They wanted a casual approach to art, hoping to show glimpses of their environment. The solid forms of Neo-classicism dissolved into the broken color and soft edges of Impressionism. The quality of light became the subject matter, rather than people, places and things. French artists Manet, Renoir, Monet, Degas and Pissarro and the American, Mary Cassatt, experimented with and directed the movement of Impressionism.

But this approach to painting was not suited to artists who wanted to emphasize form and structure

The vivid colors and slashing brushstrokes are characteristic of Vincent van Gogh's work. He used the contrasting hues and thickly-painted surfaces to express an emotional quality in his work. Portrait of a Peasant, *1888, is a 25" × 21" (65 × 54 cm) oil painting. Norton Simon Inc. Foundation, Los Angeles.*

Claude Monet created many paintings of the Rouen Cathedral in France. Each shows a different quality of light, reflecting different times of day and different seasons. Notice how the soft edges of the painting differ from the actual hard stone surface. Norton Simon Museum, Pasadena.

or convey strong emotions. A whole generation of artists (including some of the Impressionists) soon broke the restraints of Impressionism. They were still indebted, however, to the artists who showed them a new way of seeing the world.

Paul Cézanne led the way for a group of artists called Post-Impressionists. His concern for form, design and more solid compositions laid the foundation for later design-oriented painters. Gauguin used color to intensify the emotion in his work. Van Gogh expressed his own personal turmoil with bold color, textures and incredible bursts of energy. Toulouse-Lautrec echoed the flat patterns of Japanese print-making, translating them into French subject matter.

Other innovations in art also began to emerge at this time, opening the doors for the fantastic range of styles found in the twentieth century.

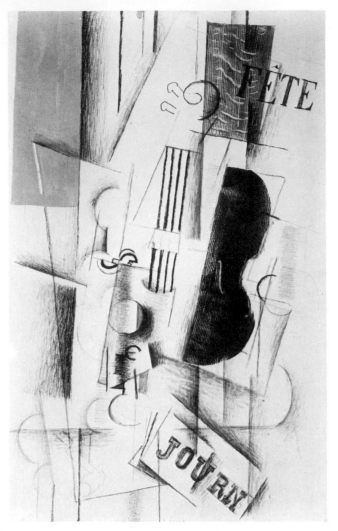

Cubism took many forms. In Musical Forms, *Georges Braque fractured the shapes of a guitar and rearranged the parts to please his own sense of design. Notice how he introduced words into the painting. Philadelphia Museum of Art.*

Pablo Picasso worked in many styles. He was one of the earliest Expressionists. His oil painting, The Tragedy, *1903, certainly leaves no doubt concerning the subject and its emotional meaning. National Gallery of Art, Washington, D.C.*

Early Twentieth Century Art

As the twentieth century began, artists could choose from a wide range of styles and techniques. Art was beginning to recognize individual differences and the artist's need for many forms of visual expression.

The *Fauvists* emphasized bright and vibrant color. The *Cubists* based their work on the geometrical organization of Cézanne. They distorted and fractured natural forms. World War I disrupted art's natural development. After the war, artists sought individual ways to communicate.

Wassily Kandinsky was the first artist to abandon recognizable subject matter in his work. Open Green, *1923, is a nonobjective painting in which the subject is the artist's arrangement of color, lines and shapes. Norton Simon Inc. Foundation, Los Angeles.*

René Magritte, a French Surrealist, painted very realistically, but he put subjects in strange combinations and situations. In Time Transfixed, *1939, the objects are easy to recognize, but their combination is not logical. Art Institute of Chicago.*

Futurists in Italy emphasized the speed and frantic activity of the machine age. The *Constructionists* in Russia rebuilt nature along geometric lines. German *Expressionists* used color and jagged shapes. *Abstractionists* began to simplify and rearrange existing forms. And, for the first time, artists painted *Non-objective* works that had no recognizable subject matter.

Frustrated with the war and society, artists in the *Dada* movement protested traditional art forms. The *Surrealists* tried to visualize the inner workings of the mind. They painted concepts and ideas instead of logical arrangements.

Such a variety of expression had never occurred before. The public had a difficult time understanding and accepting such changes. The result was a widening gap between the art world and the rest of society. As artists demanded the freedom to freely express themselves, the public became confused. They began to rely on the traditional styles that were easier to understand.

Jackson Pollock helped take America to the forefront of the Abstract Expressionist movement. His Full Fathom Five, *1947, is a 51″ × 30″ (130 × 77 cm) oil painting. He brushed, dripped and poured the paint to create a richly-textured surface. Museum of Modern Art, New York.*

Twentieth Century Art in America

During the first half of the twentieth century, American artists competed with Europeans to develop new styles and methods of art. American artists were competent and skillful, but the newest and most original ideas came from Europe. Following World War II, however, Americans such as Jackson Pollock, Hans Hoffman, Willem de Kooning and Franz Klein became leaders of *Abstract Expressionism.* They pushed American art to the forefront of avant-garde expressionism.

Americans continued to lead the way in the following years with *Pop Art* (everyday things in a simplified style), *Op Art* (optical effects), and *Color Field Painting* (large flat areas of color). Sculptors experimented with an incredible variety of new materials and techniques, including plastics, computers, holograms, lasers and video.

New Realism stressed photo-realistic approaches to subject matter. *Post-Painterly Abstraction* and *New Art* combined the freedom of Abstract Expressionism with new materials and techniques.

No single type of art dominates the contemporary scene. Instead, there are many different types of expression. This has been called *Pluralism.* Today, Artists are exploring many directions from realism to abstraction to something called Minimal Art. One artist exhibited 271 blank sheets of paper, representing 271 days on which she rejected concepts that had occurred to her.

Art has always been difficult to define. In the last part of the twentieth century we still cannot write a simple, clear definition. However, artists continue to work at personal means of expression. They continue to share their ideas and concepts with those interested and patient enough to respond to them.

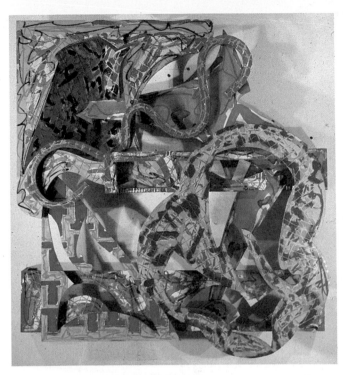

In these two works, you can see the tremendous range of contemporary visual expression. Frank Stella's *Zolder XXII*, *1982*, is a mixed-media work painted on wide strips of etched magnesium. It is 70″ × 80″ × 14″ (198 × 204 × 36 cm). Courtesy Leo Castelli Gallery, New York. Duane Hanson's Man with Crutches, *1979*, is a life-size Super Realistic sculpture created with painted polyester and fiberglass. It has real clothes and accessories. Courtesy of the artist.

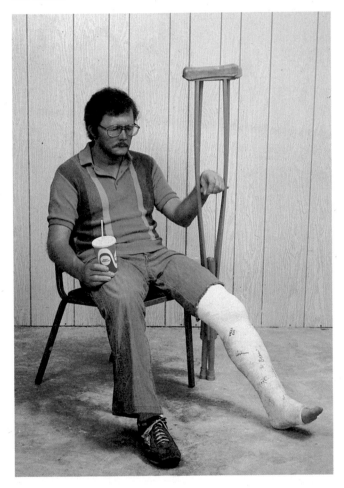

Suggested Activities

1. Visit as many museums and galleries as you can, either by yourself, with parents or friends or with your art class. Museums contain historically important art. Galleries display what is happening in art today.
2. Pick any artist whose work appears in this chapter, and research his or her life and work. Write a brief summary. Describe the artist's life and/or the artist's style and technique of work.
3. Cut pictures of paintings, sculpture and buildings from old art books. Design and arrange a visual art timeline that can be placed in a hallway or classroom. This activity works best in a group.
4. Imagine you are an artist, living in a previous century. Select a time when you would have liked to live and be an artist. Write a short description about the kind of art you would make and why you would enjoy living and working at that time.

5 Looking at Art: What Does It Say?

We have seen how art is constructed (designed) and how it has developed from simple crafted items and paintings to sophisticated visual statements. We have studied art from the artists' point of view. In this chapter, we will look at art from the other side. How can the viewer complete the process of communication? How can we learn to live with art and begin to understand what artists are saying?

Art begins with an idea. A landscape theme is only one of many possible ideas for art. Once *landscape* is chosen, the artist decides what to say and how to say it. This is the *concept,* the reason for making the art. What will the artist communicate about the landscape? A specific place, remembered scene, impression or idea related to the landscape?

Every artist has a personal reason for making his or her art. As viewers, it is up to us to look, enjoy and receive the visual images. Only then is the communication process complete. We might see immediately what the artist wanted to tell us or we might need time before we understand the work. Sometimes the message is unclear, or we might see and feel something that the artist did not intend. That is fine, because we read the visual message from the perspective of our background and experiences. We cannot all see and feel the same thing in every work of art.

Look at the five landscapes shown here. Notice the different concepts, purposes and styles of each artist. Each has worked with a landscape theme. Each started with a different concept, used a personal style and expressed a definite idea about landscape.

Carole D. Barnes. Winter Reds. *Acrylic and collage, 29" × 35" (74 × 89 cm).*

All are valid, truthful and personally satisfying visual statements.

Try to see what the artists saw in each landscape. What did they tell us about their landscapes? Why do you like one more than another? What was each artist's purpose? Can you see what each one was excited about? Are there features in some that can be compared to others? Did the artists succeed in making you think more intensely about landscapes? Have your own concepts of landscape expanded? Will you look at the natural environment differently now? What have you learned about your own likes and dislikes in art? Your own artistic expression?

Clare Romano. Grand Canyon. *12-color collagraph, 7-piece segmented plate, 22" × 30" (56 × 76 cm).*

Arthur Secunda. Lugano Suite # 16. Serigraph, *34.5" × 23" (87 × 58 cm).*

Nanci B. Closson. Color Series. Acrylic on canvas, *64" × 50" (162 × 128 cm).*

Gerald F. Brommer. Sierra Stream. *Watercolor and collage, 15" × 22" (38 × 56 cm).*

François Millet. The Gleaners, *1948. Oil on canvas, 21″ × 26″ (53 × 66 cm). The Louvre, Paris.*

Content and Concept in Art

Study the three works on these pages. One was done in 1848, the other two more recently. One piece is a sculpture and two are oil paintings. Despite all the obvious differences, there is one similarity: *content.* Each artist has chosen the same subject matter—men and women in their *environment.* Each work shows people living at the same time as the artists, doing ordinary, everyday things in a group. Each person, however, is separated from others in the group.

The three women in Millet's painting are picking up grains of wheat after the harvesters have gone over the field. The five people in Colleen Browning's painting are riding home from work in a graffiti-covered, New York City subway. The three people in George Segal's plaster sculpture are standing on a street corner, waiting for the light to change. The content of the three works is similar, although they do not look alike.

What was each artist saying about the people? Why did they choose this subject and present it the

way they did? What insights are shared with us? The answer to these questions is the *concept* behind each work.

Francois Millet puts his three women in a sunlit field. He could have emphasized the farm workers or the horses or the texture of the straw. But he chooses to show us the determination of people to survive by working hard, even under difficult conditions. The three women are bent over. The work is hard but honorable. The results of their work are minimal. The people are poor. Millet makes the women important. He gives them stature and dignity. They are large, real and honest—they will be tired but satisfied when their day is over.

Colleen Browning places her five people (they are actually portraits of her neighbors) in a subway car. She could have shown us the inside of the car or a brand new car with clean windows. Instead, we see subway graffiti. This scene (windows, portraits, graffiti) is a kind of moving, changing mural. The artist freezes this mural for us to see and study. It is a very

Colleen Browning. Wow Car, *1978. Oil on canvas, 36" × 54" (91 × 188 cm). Kennedy Galleries, New York.*

realistic picture. Browning explores the concept of embedding people in her painting. She shares her contemporary surroundings with us and makes a statement about life in New York City. She shows us the creative side of subway vandalism and allows us to think about it in a different way. The concept is a challenging one.

George Segal puts plaster casts of real people in natural situations. He could have shown us heroes, presidents or movie stars. But he chooses to work with ordinary people. The people are standing on a street corner, a sight we have seen hundreds of times. Why show us such common things? The "Walk/Don't Walk" sign is real. It flashes and changes. What has that got to do with art? When the artist puts all the elements together we see a strikingly familiar theme. He shows us loneliness on a crowded street corner. Each person is preoccupied with his or her own thoughts. The flashing sign controls our movement. We wait and then we move on. We become part of the art as we study the sculpture.

George Segal. Walk, Don't Walk, *1976. Plaster, cement, painted wood and electric light, 104" × 72" × 72" (267 × 182 × 182 cm). Whitney Museum of American Art, New York.*

Norman Rockwell. The New Television Set, *1949. Oil on canvas, 53" × 42" (136 × 108 cm). Los Angeles County Museum of Art.*

Subject Matter and Style

When you are ready to draw, paint or make other kinds of art, the first question is "What shall I make?" The answer to that question (a house, cat or tree) is the subject matter or content of your artwork. Subject matter is what the art is about. Most artists use *things* as their subject matter (such as apples, people, cars, trees or animals). Others use *ideas* such as joy, love, loneliness or frustration. Others are concerned with the scientific or *mathematical aspects* of art (design and proportions). These concepts can also be subject matter.

Subject matter and *content* refer to *what* can be seen by looking at the work. *Concept* refers to *why* and *how* the art was designed and produced. *Technique* refers to the *way* it is made or put together. *Style* refers to the artist's *individual approach* to subject, content and technique.

There are many subjects to choose from. The ways of dealing with them are endless. Some examples are described briefly below. You can look through the book and find many more.

Narrative subjects—tell a story; either the artist's or someone else's (see the Norman Rockwell painting).

Literary subjects—visually describe (illustrate) a book, short story or poem.

Religious subjects—visualize ideas, beliefs and stories from religious writings and teachings.

Landscapes—artwork about the natural environment (mountains, lakes, seashores, meadows).

Cityscapes—views of the urban environment (streets, buildings, crowds).

Historical subjects—scenes from history (battles, treaties, explorations, discoveries).

Figures—art based on human figures from mythology, history or contemporary life.

Portraits—close-up views, usually of one or a few people. May be full length, bust (head and shoulders) or facial.

Self-portraits—paintings or drawings that artists make of themselves.

Genre subjects—normal, everyday activities (cooking, shopping, reading).

Social comment—visual statements about political views, religion, civil rights; criticism of events, ideas or actions.

Still lifes—inanimate subjects in paintings or drawings (bowls, bottles, fruit, fabrics).

Emotional expressions—art that emphasizes the

Stuart Davis. *Something on the Eight Ball, 1954. Oil on canvas, 56″ × 45″ (142 × 114 cm). Philadelphia Museum of Art.*

Richard Estes. *Drugstore, 1970. Oil on canvas, 44″ × 60″ (113 × 152 cm). The Art Institute of Chicago.*

feelings of the artists toward the subjects, rather than realistic presentations.

Abstraction—simplifies subjects to several basic shapes, lines and/or colors.

Non-objective art—emphasizes the color, line, movement, shape or design of the art, without using recognizable objects.

Of course, there are other subjects and styles but this list gives an idea of the range of options artists have today.

Study the three paintings shown here. All deal with the urban environment, but each artist treats the subject differently. Norman Rockwell tells us a story about fixing a television antenna. Richard Estes paints a cool, accurate and realistic work about a corner drugstore in his city. Stuart Davis paints the

Arthur Secunda. Lugano Suite #5, *1983. Serigraph, 34″ × 25″ (86 × 64 cm).*

lights, signs, color and excitement of his city and expresses ideas without using buildings and people. The style becomes characteristic of the artist. If you saw other works by these artists, you could probably recognize which one made each painting.

Intellect and Emotion in Art

Throughout the history of art, there are two extremes of expression. One is a completely emotional approach with no concern for design and reason. The other is a completely intellectual approach without feeling and emotion. A few artists work at one or the other of the two extremes. But, most people possess both qualities (although one may be stronger than the other). If you like art to be full of action and express feelings, you are probably on the emotional side of the scale. If you like art to be perfect, cool and calculated, you probably lean toward the intellectual approach.

Study the art shown here and notice how the emphasis varies from work to work. Features typical of

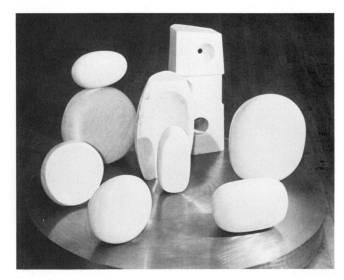

Barbara Hepworth. Assembly of Sea Forms, *1972. White marble, tallest form 33″ (84 cm). Norton Simon Museum of Art, Pasadena.*

Charles Burchfield. Sun and Rocks, *1950. Watercolor on paper, 40" × 56" (102 × 142 cm). Albright-Knox Art Gallery, Buffalo.*

Hugo Robus. Despair, *1927. Bronze, 12" (30 cm). Whitney Museum of American Art, New York.*

an intellectual (or classic) approach are: emphasis on design and composition; a cool, calculated approach to the subjects; emphasis on neat, clean arrangements and proportions and excellent drawing skills.

Features typical of an emotional (or romantic) approach are: an active and colorful treatment of the subjects; violent movement; distortion and emphasis on personal feelings.

Compare and contrast the two landscape paintings and the two sculptures. Then compare the Barbara Hepworth and Arthur Secunda works, and the Charles Burchfield and Hugo Robus works. How are they alike and how are they different? What was each artist trying to say? How did they communicate their thoughts and ideas? Which artists are expressionistic and which are intellectual?

Do you think you could recognize other works by these artists? How is the content of the two paintings alike? Different?

These works are obvious examples of the two different approaches. Which approach (intellectual or emotional) do you like better? If you made a landscape painting right now, which style would you try? Or would you combine both approaches? Your answers will tell you something about yourself and your own feelings about art and life.

What Do Artists Have to Say to Us?

On the next few pages, you can study the work of several artists to see how they communicate through their art. Some express ideas about their ethnic cultures, their families, contemporary life, cities or their feelings. Answering the questions about each work will help you understand a few of the artists' ideas. Perhaps you can make up questions of your own to ask your classmates.

Mexican Landscape
by José Clemente Orozco. Mexican, about 1930.

Even when José Clemente Orozco created a small painting (this one is only 37 inches wide), it looked like a mural. His style uses large simplified forms. He shaded the forms to give a solid three-dimensional feeling. Most of Orozco's work was done on walls in some of the larger Mexican cities. After the revolution in 1910, Orozco and his fellow artists (including Diego Rivera and David Siqueros) covered many public walls with murals. Their paintings expressed strong political feelings. They often expressed sympathy for the poor people of Mexico.

Orozco's *Mexican Landscape* has a similar message. What do you see in the painting? The cactus plant is called the "maguey." It is a main source of food, drink, cloth, rope and other items for the desert people. How did Orozco show the importance of the plant? How can you tell that the plant is used? What kind of mood did the artist develop? How do you feel toward the people? Do they have enough food?

How did Orozco use values to dramatize his work? Notice how he united the plant and the people in a common shape. Why did he do this? How is the painting balanced? Can you find repeated shapes? Is the light realistic or controlled by the artist? How did he simplify the forms of the people and the plant? Was he successful in stating his ideas and feelings?

Spring Way
by Romare Bearden. American, 1964.
What medium did the artist use in this work? Is collage an old or new medium? Where did the artist get the materials for this work?

Romare Bearden has a strong message to communicate. He lived in the crowded tenements of New York. He wants you to see its problems and frustrations. Years ago, he chose collage as his medium. He developed it into a very effective style. Why might collage be more effective than oil painting?

What can you tell about where the artist lived by looking at *Spring Way?* How does the painting show this to you? How much sky do you see? How many trees? How much lawn? How much empty space? Is Bearden's style effctive?

Explain the organization of shapes and lines in this work. Do you see the repeated shapes and values? Which shape is used most? Why? Where can you see the variety of textures and values? Is the painting flat or are there places where you can get *into* it?

There are two figures in the collage. Can you describe them? Why did Bearden show them this way? Are they dominated by the structures? Notice how some sections of the collage are very abstract or non-objective. Why do you think the artist did this? Did he communicate his message to you?

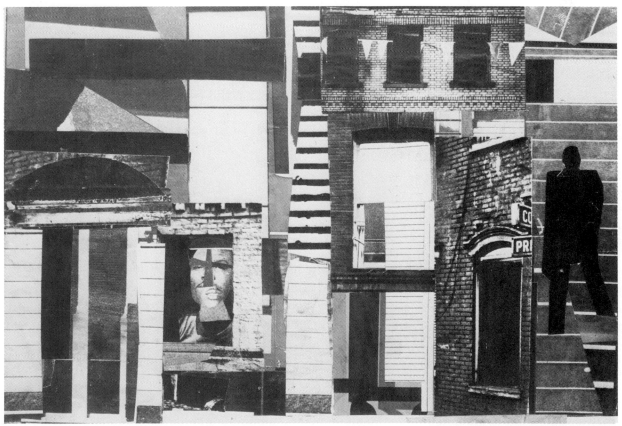

Courtesy of the artist, Romare Bearden.

Prado Museum, Madrid, Spain.

Artists often want to share their thoughts about things that are important to them. These ideas may deal with personal or equal rights, ethnic concerns, religious beliefs, contemporary culture or favorite activities and pastimes. El Greco was a very religious artist. His beliefs are clearly communicated in his art. Thomas Eakins loved all types of sports. Although he painted many other subjects, he enjoyed painting his friends as they played sports. What activities interest you? Have you ever thought about drawing or painting them?

The Resurrection
by El Greco. Spanish, about 1590.
El Greco's real name was Domenikos Theotokopoulos. He was born in Crete (Greece), but spent most of his life in Spain, where he was called El Greco (the Greek). He was a deeply religious man. Most of his paintings reflect his beliefs. *The Resurrection* is one of these. It shows Christ bursting from his tomb with the banner of victory.

Did El Greco paint his figures realistically, as Renaissance artists did? In most of his paintings, the figures are stretched into tall thin forms. He did this to express his feelings about humans trying to reach up toward heaven.

In what direction does your eye move in this work? How did El Greco use value, shape and line to direct your eye? Where is the center of interest?

The painting is divided into two parts. There is peace and glory in the upper half, confusion and furious action in the lower part. Find places of contrasting values. Most of El Greco's paintings have this vertical feeling of reaching upward.

How did he show the confusion of the soldiers? Notice how he designed the figures so that feet, legs and hands seem to fit the spaces. Is this realism? Is the light realistic? The flickering quality of light, controlled by the artist, is another characteristic of El Greco's style.

The Biglen Brothers Racing
by Thomas Eakins. American, 1873.

One of Thomas Eakins favorite sports to paint was rowing, or sculling. He also painted baseball players, swimmers and wrestlers, as well as portraits. Here he shows his two friends, the Biglen brothers, winning a race on the river. Is the main eye movement horizontal or vertical? How does this help strengthen the action of the rowers?

Eakins painted in the Realist style. He tried to use real colors and textures to paint people and places. He did not add drama or mystery to his work, or his personal feelings. He spent many hours studying reflections on the water and the anatomy of the human body, so he could paint them realistically.

Is this painting quiet and still or full of action? How did Eakins emphasize the two rowers? How did he show depth in the painting? Look at the shadows on the figures. How do they help the two men appear to be three-dimensional? Eakins often made small clay models of people and placed them in miniature sculls (boats). He did this so he could see *exactly* how the light and shadow appeared on them. Eakins was the first artist to use motion pictures to study the way muscles look in action. How does this knowledge and preparation show up in the painting?

National Gallery of Art, Washington, D.C. (Gift of Mr. and Mrs. Cornelius Vanderbilt Whitney).

Some artists make visual statements that express their personal concerns about contemporary culture. Such art may call attention to political or cultural circumstances, or it may show fads or current interests. The three works shown here are personal responses to our times.

Computer Cosmology
by Colleen Browning. American, 1980.
This interesting painting is Colleen Browning's idea of a new and different universe. It is like looking up at a starry night, but all the elements in the painting are not natural.

The title provides a clue to understanding the work. Computers are now part of our daily lives. (Can you imagine how people in 1825 or 1925 would have reacted to this painting?) This is not a painting of part of a computer. It is an idea **based on** computer circuits and elements. The word **cosmology** refers to ideas about the form and function of the universe.

What techniques did the artist use to give the feeling of deep space? Where have you seen some of the lines and shapes before? Do you feel electricity and power in the painting? Do you feel movement? How does the artist communicate this to you? How does she use values? How does the painting tell us about three-dimensional space?

Can you think of other ways to dramatize the role of computers in our lives?

The Dinner Party
by Judy Chicago. American, 1979.
Judy Chicago likes to work on huge art projects. Over 400 people from across the country helped her finish and display this work. *The Dinner Party* is a gigantic production, made of china-painted porcelain and different kinds of needlework. The work symbolizes the history of women in Western civilization.

The work is triangular shaped in the form of a huge banquet table, 48' on each side. The place settings symbolize forty of the most important women in the world. Many of these women are not in history books. The tile floor is inscribed with the names of more than 1,000 other important women who have received little attention.

The gigantic work needs a huge museum space to be exhibited. Is there a room in your school that is big enough for it? The artist wants *The Dinner Party* to be shown in major museums. She wants many people to get her message that women **are** important contributors to the world's cultural development. The piece can be broken down into many smaller parts, but shipping it is still a big moving and storage project.

Courtesy of the artist.

Collection of Leo Castelli, New York.

The work itself cannot be bought, but the artist sells books and films that illustrate the entire project, from her initial idea to the final display.

Masterpiece
by Roy Lichtenstein. American, 1962.
Have you seen pictures like this before? This large square painting is 54" on each side. It is done in oil on canvas. Does it look like any other painting you have seen? Roy Lichtenstein works in a style called Pop Art. He became interested in using the comic strip for a subject when he painted a Mickey Mouse for his son.

Have you ever looked at newspaper pictures with a magnifying glass? Try it. The grays in each photo or comic strip are made up of many little dots. This is done so that a machine can print the correct values. Lichtenstein decided to combine the simplified comic strip technique with this printing technique. He developed his own style. He gives us a new and different view of our machine age. He often silkscreens the dot patterns on his paintings.

Can you see how the artist develops a style that expresses a message? What is Roy Lichtenstein telling us about our times? Cézanne wanted you to see his brush strokes. Can you see any brushstrokes in Lichtenstein's work? Why do you think he doesn't want you to see them? Is the artist's message in the words or in the style of the painting? Pop Art usually tries to make us see ourselves more clearly. Is Lichtenstein's message social criticism or is it just fun?

95

The next three paintings deal with the city. Look at the dates when the paintings were made. Buildings and streets may not change much, but these artists certainly have different styles.

The Piazetta, Venice, Looking North
by Giovanni Canaletto. Italian, 1755.
Canaletto lived in Venice and loved to paint its buildings, canals and city squares. His exact use of detail gives us an accurate picture of his Venice. The painting looks like a photograph! The artist painted it very carefully. At that time, many people from Northern Europe traveled south to Italy and Venice. They wanted to take reminders of home. Several painters provided realistic paintings of their cities.

Notice the exact detail in the buildings and people. All of the buildings in the painting are still standing. The piazetta looks very much the same here as it does today. Only the style of people's clothing has changed. How did the artist create a feeling of depth? Why are the people important in the painting? From what direction is the sunshine coming? What other details can you find?

It is impossible to actually see the view shown in the painting unless you are in a balloon, hovering over the water, or standing on the deck of a large ship. How do you think the artist prepared for this work? How did he make a picture from this viewpoint? Why is drawing important to Canaletto? How is this painting similar to and different from the other two?

Cityscape I
by Richard Diebenkorn. American, 1963
Many of Richard Diebenkorn's paintings are more abstract than this one. His subjects are often elements of the city. *Cityscape* shows us part of a city. It emphasizes the patterns and shapes produced by structures and their shadows.

Norton Simon Foundation, Los Angeles.

Is this the middle of a city or the suburbs? How can you tell? Is the land flat or hilly? Is it summer or winter? Is it noontime? Why or why not? How does the artist show depth and space in this painting? What seems more important, depth or pattern?

Compare Diebenkorn's use of perspective with the other two paintings. How is Diebenkorn's work similar to and different from Feininger's? Is *Cityscape I* more or less expressionistic than the other two? Why?

Can you explain every part of this work? Is detail as important to Diebenkorn as it is to Canaletto?

Notice that all artists do not see the same things. They interpret subject matter in their own personal ways.

Zirchon VII
by Lyonel Feininger. American, 1912.

Lyonel Feininger made a living drawing cartoons for the comic section of newspapers. But painting also interested him. Sailboats and buildings were his favorite subjects. Feininger was born in the United States, but he spent much of his early life in Germany.

Churches and other public buildings are often the subjects of Feininger's paintings. Can you find the buildings in this painting of a German city? Can you describe Feininger's style?

Feininger's paintings are divided into simple geometric shapes. He starts with actual buildings, but paints them in his own style. How do the sizes of the shapes stress variety? Can you see how the artist extended some lines from the buildings to create new shapes? This is a Cubist technique, but Feininger used it to fit his own style.

How did he add interest and excitement to the painting? Is the painting emotional or carefully designed? Are the shapes natural or geometrical? How can you tell that Feininger is not concerned with your feelings about the city? Is he more concerned with its geometry and structure?

The Museum of Modern Art, New York. (Gift of Walter P. Chrysler, Jr.).

The Studio

by Pablo Picasso. Spanish, 1928.

Study Pablo Picasso's **The Studio.** The painting, done in 1928, is an abstract work. Objects are painted in very simplified shapes, lines and colors. The artist is at the left, working at his easel. How many eyes does he have? What was Picasso's reason for showing three eyes? Can you see the easel?

The studio interior is on the right. Can you find the table covered with a draped cloth? Do you see the fruit bowl with an apple in it? Find the painting on the wall. Notice how everything is simplified. The whitish object is a plaster sculpture on the table.

Which art elements has Picasso emphasized? Do the objects look real? Does space seem flat or deep? Picasso also painted realistically but he chose an abstract style for this work. Notice how he designed edges and shapes to relate to each other.

Suggested Activities

1. Study the list of possible subject matter in the section on subject matter and style in this chapter. Look through the book and find two or three examples of each. List each example by artist, title of work, medium and size (if available).

2. It is important to understand that some artists communicate strong personal interests. Look through magazines and collect fifteen or twenty illustrations that relate to your special interests. Arrange them in a notebook for visual reference.

3. Choose several works of art (from this book or from prints or slides). Write five questions about each one, similar to the questions asked in this chapter. The questions will help you better understand the works.

4. Choose two painters from another chapter in the book. Write a paragraph about each. Discuss subject, style, medium, color, visual message and your feelings and reactions.

Creating Art

6 Drawing: A Record of What You See

A little child picks up a crayon and starts to scribble on the floor. A top fashion designer takes a pencil and begins recording ideas on paper. A well-known artist, on a sketching trip, puts down lines and shapes, shadows and forms. An industrial designer, working on ideas for a new telephone, jots down ideas and notes that will be used in finished drawings. All these people, from the three year old to the top designers, are doing the same thing—they are all drawing.

Drawing is the basic activity of art. It is the recording of things that you see. It is a way of communicating to others the ideas and thoughts, the sights and experiences that are important to you. Drawing is a way of seeing. It can be careful and studied, or quick and sketchy.

Drawings have been made on cave walls, animal skins, papyrus, wood, paper, ceramic panels and canvas. Drawings have been made with charcoal, lead and sticks dipped in color. They have also been made with silver-tipped rods, pens, brushes, reeds and quills. After many centuries of art, drawing is still a basic skill. No matter how accomplished an artist is, he must still draw to plan and produce his art.

The work on these pages shows a variety of drawing materials and techniques. Some of the pieces are sketches for later paintings; others are completely finished work. Some use pencil, while others use computers. You can learn a lot by looking at the drawings of artists who lived before you. You can also learn from the work of artists today.

Developing Your Own Drawing Style

Vincent van Gogh, Paul Cézanne, Leonardo da Vinci, Francisco Goya and Ausguste Renoir are all great names in the art world, even though they lived a long time ago. Each had a style that set him apart from other artists. After a little study, you probably could pick out a van Gogh drawing from a group of works. Today's artists also have their own drawing styles, just as they have different styles of handwriting or talking. Drawing is a very personal way of expressing yourself. You should draw in your own style. This means that your work should be unique—not like the work of anyone else. But how do you get your own style?

You don't really look for a style. It develops out of your experiences. Every time you look at something carefully to record it, you are working on your style. You might experiment and try working in the style of van Gogh, Renoir or Goya. They can give you ideas

A drawing is often a search for information. It need not be completed if the artist is satisfied with the search. Turkey Buzzard *by Andrew Wyeth is a study from life, drawn in pencil. Collection of the Museum of Fine Arts, Boston (M. Karouk bequest).*

Lyonel Feininger sketched this full-rigged ship in ink on scratch paper. Then he added ink washes and watercolor. This sketch is an idea for a future painting. Notice how the style of his drawing is similar to that of his painting (see page 97). Norton Simon Museum, Pasadena.

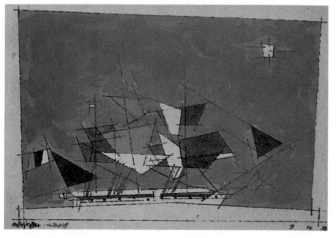

When you draw, look carefully at your subject. Then add lines or values to your paper.

for your own style. You learn something by looking at other drawings, but you learn more about drawing by drawing.

You can tell who wrote the last letter you got because you recognize the handwriting. Your teacher knows your handwriting. She can tell whose paper is on the desk, even if no name is on it. Your drawing should be as easily recognized. If the entire class is drawing from a still life or from a student model, each student's drawing should be different from the others. You look at a subject and draw it in your own way. Your neighbor might see the same subject differently and draw it in another, slightly different,

Leonardo da Vinci made this drawing as a study before he began one of his major paintings. It shows the pleasant smile and shading technique that are found in many of his paintings. The Metropolitan Museum of Art, New York (Harris Brisbane Dick Fund).

This sketch from 1944 shows the simplified linear style of Henri Matisse. Notice how his line and the shading technique of Leonardo (above) differ. Each drawing represents the artist's personal style. Los Angeles County Museum of Art.

way. Each artist shown on these pages has a personal drawing style.

Everything you look at, every experience you have and every drawing you make helps produce your style. The drawings you look at, the magazines you read, and the teachers you have also influence your style. How can visits to museums, summer vacations or a careful study of a flower affect your style? Can you see that your style is a result of all your visual experiences? Your individual drawing (and painting) style should not be like someone else's. Your drawings should be as personal as your handwriting or voice.

If you concentrate on looking carefully, selecting what you want to show and putting it down in your own way, your style will begin to develop. The following activities should help you develop skills in both looking and drawing. Work in as many ways as possible, using all the materials available, and your own style will begin to appear.

Francis de Erdely's drawing style is easy to recognize. He enlarges a bit here, distorts a bit there and uses line and value in a unique way. This drawing was made with ink and pens, sticks and flat pieces of balsa wood.

Contemporary artists also seek styles of their own. They experiment constantly. Channa Davies Horwitz used ink on graph paper to create And Then There Were None, #3. *Can you follow the progression from beginning to end? Courtesy Orlando Gallery, Encino, California.*

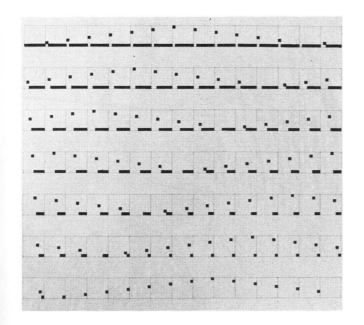

103

Drawing Tools and Techniques

You may have already worked with a variety of drawing materials. You probably have used more tools than were available to great artists such as Raphael or Leonardo da Vinci. Today there is a large variety of drawing materials. We can place them into three groups: dry media, wet media and mixed media. You should try to use some materials from each group. Try some on different papers, from smooth to very textured, and see the results.

The *dry media* include pencils, charcoal, chalk, crayon materials and scratchboard. *Pencils* are the basic tool in the dry media. They come in a wide range of values (light to dark) and sizes (thin to wide and flat). Because pencils are easy to carry, they are a favorite sketching tool. You can use the tip of a pencil to make a thin line. Or you can use the side of the lead to shade softly. Dull pencils make wide soft marks. Sharpened pencils make thin hard lines. Pencils with thick lead can be sharpened to a chisel point to make still different marks.

You should try several kinds of pencils on several kinds of paper to see the different marks you can make. Pencil drawings can be delicate or bold, sketchy or finished. Different pressure of your hand (heavy or light) will cause the same pencil to make different marks. Pencil lines can be erased with several types of erasers, but too much rubbing will chew up the paper.

Charcoal is the driest and dustiest of the dry media. It is the oldest drawing tool. Can you figure out why? Like pencils, charcoal comes in many different values and hardnesses. It also comes in pencil form, as compressed sticks or in natural stick form. Try several so you know what works best for you.

Charcoal can be smudged and smoothed with your fingers or a scrap of soft cloth. It is a powdery material. It must be sprayed with a fixative to make it

Pencils can make lines and shading, as this student demonstrates. Can you make similar drawings of a leaf, flower or toy?

Charcoal is excellent for shading and for showing the form of objects. A student first sketched the outlines of this still life and then added the shading by drawing and smudging.

stick to the paper. Because of this powdery quality, the paper needs to be slightly textured for best results. If you use charcoal, try holding the stick in different ways, until it feels comfortable. Kneaded rubber erasers are used to clean up smudges or erase mistaken lines or shapes.

Chalk is similar to charcoal in texture, but it comes in a wide variety of colors. A fixative is needed to make it stick permanently to paper. You can use chalk dry, or you can dip it in water or liquid starch before putting it on paper. Experiment a little to see how you can get different results.

Wax crayons are old friends—you have used them for many years. They can be used to make delicately shaded drawings or strong, bold statements. They can be blended by rubbing with squares of paper. Or they can be scratched off the paper. They can be used with watercolor or ink in a resist technique. Finished work can be slightly melted with a warm iron. You can use the sides or the tips of crayons for a variety of shading or line techniques. They can be used to make rubbings by placing paper over a textured surface and rubbing with the flat side of the crayon. Fill several pages with experiments that show many ways crayons can be used.

Black and white crayons were used to create this drawing of a musical instrument. Colored construction paper adds color to a drawing and provides a middle value.

This student self-portrait was done in crayon. Notice the very simple lines and shapes. Can you use this approach to make a self-portrait?

While some artists prefer the dry media for their drawings, others would rather work with the **wet media.** These materials are permanent and erasing is almost impossible.

Ink is the most common of the wet media. It comes in colors as well as in black (called India ink). It can be diluted with water to make **washes.** Washes are lighter in value than the original ink. The more water, the lighter the value.

Ink can be put on paper with many different tools. **Steel pens** are probably the most common. Pens come in a variety of sizes and shapes, from small and thin to wide and flat. Some can be used for fine line work, while others fill in large areas. Try several, to see the marks that each one makes. Ink can also be put down with reed pens, bamboo pens, or unusual tools such as sticks, twigs or cardboard pieces.

Inks (full strength or diluted) can also be put on paper with brushes of any size or shape. If diluted, the work is called a **wash drawing.** Wash drawings use several values of gray. Often, wash drawings are painted loosely and may use a line to outline the forms.

Wet media are also available in many kinds of self-contained tools. Fountain pens, ball-point pens, felt-tipped and fiber-tipped pens and markers are easy to carry, ready for instant use and are excellent tools for sketching.

While the gray washes are still damp on the oatmeal paper, this student is using a bamboo pen to run black ink lines into the wash drawing.

Pen and ink (black) and colored markers were combined in this student drawing of umbrellas. The ink lines were drawn first. They were carefully designed and placed.

Selecting the right paper for each of the wet media is important. Pens work best on smooth paper; wash drawings on textured paper. Experiment on scraps to see which works best in each case.

Some artists prefer to work in a single medium, such as charcoal or ink. But others like to experiment, using several different media in the same drawing. *Mixed-media* drawings can produce exciting results, usually with rich textural surfaces.

Dry materials, such as pencil, crayon or charcoal, can be mixed together. Wet materials can also be mixed—try a wash drawing with charcoal and ink lines. The most exciting combinations use wet and dry media together, such as white wax crayon and wash drawing. You can experiment with all sorts of combinations and on all kinds of papers to see what textures you can get. You might even paste paper scraps into your work to get more surface variety. Today's artists like to experiment. Try several combinations to make your work more interesting.

Charles White was a master at drawing. This portrait study is a wash drawing, brushed on with different values of brown inks. Emphasis lines were added with black ink and a pen. Notice the variety of textures and values.

White crayon and dark ink washes were used in this mixed-media fish. Rich textures can be created with several layers of crayon and wash.

Some Design Suggestions

The first question most drawing students ask is, "How do I start?" There are many ways to get going, but this three-step plan is easiest.

1. Look at the *large shapes* first, not at the details. Sketch these into place lightly. This gives you a visual outline in which to work. Keep your outline simple and look for relationships of size and position of parts.
2. Develop your sketch by correcting the lines and adding some major details. Eliminate unwanted material and concentrate on the major forms.
3. Begin to shade, texture or color according to your ideas for that drawing and its medium.

Look back through the section on design to refresh your memory on the elements and principles that can be applied to drawing. Line is the basic element used in drawing, but shape, value, texture, space and color are also important. The principles of balance, unity, emphasis, contrast, pattern, movement and rhythm are as important to good drawing as to fine painting or sculpture.

Explore various materials and techniques to see what each will do. Some produce better line. Others make textures more easily. You will begin to understand which material is best suited to each subject as you experiment with them.

Look carefully as you draw. Looking is as important as putting lines on paper. Draw what you *see* and *feel,* rather than what you think you know. The drawing ideas that follow will help you explore many materials and subject matter. This will help you understand yourself better. You will begin to see which are your favorite subjects and working methods.

Even a complicated still life should be simplified into a few large shapes first. This makes it easier to put the parts in correct relationship to each other. Then the shading and detail can be added.

You can draw from your environment. This student pen and ink sketch was inspired by a downtown area.

What Can You Draw?

Subject matter for drawing is unlimited. John Constable, an early nineteenth century English artist, worked all his life within several miles of his home. He drew and painted the people, landscapes, seascapes and sky of his immediate environment. You can do the same thing.

Your classroom is full of subject matter, including your classmates. Keep in mind that people are subject matter, just as the vases or flowers in a still life are subject matter. Look at the model carefully and draw what you see, not what you think it should look like. Do not worry about actual likenesses. Be concerned mostly about the process of *looking* and then putting down lines, edges and values.

Have models wear unusual costumes, or have them doing something—playing a musical instrument, reading a book or hoeing the garden. This adds interest to your work and helps you make a more exciting drawing.

Gather materials for a still life. Simple arrangements are best. Arrange a variety of sizes and shapes, colors and textures to add interest to the work. Use a single strong light to see the shadows and emphasize the dark and light values.

People, places and things in your school and your neighborhood are suitable subject matter. You can draw things from close up or from a distance. Shade subjects realistically or in a stylized way. You might use a single medium or you might mix your materials.

You can use nature as your source of information, or your imagination. You might do research (looking in books, magazines or other sources) to find material from which to work. A museum visit or a field trip can provide good information.

Perhaps something you have read will spark your imagination. You may even illustrate your own writing.

Large, simple shapes and lines were put down based on a student model. The overlapping lines created shapes that are being filled with different pen and ink textures.

Bicycles, mechanical parts of machines, parks, trees and animals are waiting to be drawn. Monsters and scenes in your imagination are waiting to be recorded for others to see. It is important to remember that **careful looking**—either at **things** or **into** your imagination—is basic to drawing well.

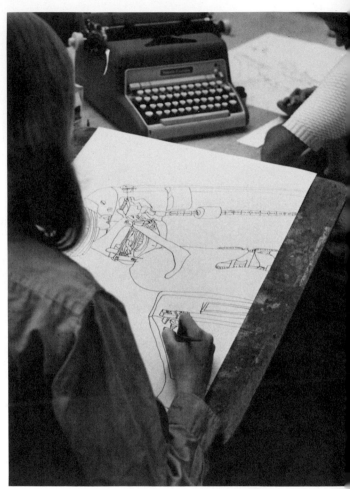

Contour drawing of mechanical objects is good practice in making us more aware of edges, details and complex relationships. This one is being done in pen and ink.

After completion of the contour drawing of this inverted tricycle, the negative spaces were filled in with brush and ink. Notice the strikingly bold result.

Sketching and Sketchbooks

Most artists who paint landscapes like to sketch. They fill sketchbooks with records of their travels and the things they see. They record trees, houses, people and animals in the way that other people keep diaries. One is *visual* notetaking, the other *verbal*.

Most painters make use of sketching. Even sculptors, architects, craftspersons and designers sketch before they begin their work.

Sketching is a way of quickly putting down ideas and sights that can be used later. Sketches are usually not thought of as artwork, however, because they will probably not be seen by anyone but the artist. They are used as sources of information for finished work.

Artists have been known to sketch on napkins, tablecloths, newspapers, sidewalks or anything available. One way to keep your sketches is to put them in a *sketchbook*. You can use your sketchbook for notes, ideas and drawings.

Sketchbooks are also excellent places to practice sketching. It is your source book. Is there a way to make your own sketchbook, rather than buy one?

Sketches might be the doodles you make while talking on the phone. Sketch your hands and feet. Look in a mirror and sketch yourself. Sketch your neighborhood, your relatives, your teacher. Quickly, without details.

Pencils, ball-point pens and markers are excellent tools for sketching. They are easy to carry and can be used immediately. Sketching is practice in *seeing* and putting down what you see. Look carefully and sketch quickly. Some sketches may take you only two or three minutes.

A trip to a museum can provide new subjects for your sketchbook. A student sketched these animals from a habitat group of African antelope.

Landscape artist Robert E. Wood fills several sketchbooks every year. You can see his variety of subjects and media.

Black crayon lines outline the vase and flowers, while white crayon lines provide textural interest. Construction paper provides a neutral colored background.

Artist George James used ink lines to create outlines and textures. Notice how some lines are heavier to emphasize certain edges.

Line—the Basic Element

Pick up any drawing tool and mark with it. You probably made a line. How many kinds of lines can you make with a pencil? Now try a brush and ink and see how many lines you can make. Did you include lines that are wiggly, broken, thin, jagged and varied? Were some straight and others curved or wiggly?

You have been making lines from the moment you began to draw. You use lines when you write words and when you drag a stick in the sand. Can you think of other kinds of lines that you make almost every day?

You can use one line to make an outline or many lines to create a feeling of shadow or solidity. Lines can show grass, leaves, clouds, hair or wrinkles in paper. Lines can outline animals and separate colors. They can express action and lead your eye to a center of interest.

Use a dark pencil to make an outline drawing (*contour drawing*) of a classmate. Keep the drawing simple and do not shade it. Work for only a few minutes. Make the lines continuous by trying to sketch without lifting the pencil from the paper. Let your eye run over the contour (edge), and let your pencil follow the same path on the paper.

Outline simple still life subjects with a light pencil line. Use pen and ink to shade the drawing with vertical lines. How can you use line in this way to show shadow and light? You may want to use pencil instead of pen and ink.

Use a brightly colored crayon to create a *line pattern* of repeated shapes on paper. A paper stencil can help you repeat certain shapes. When you are done, wash over the drawing with a complementary or dark color of watercolor in a wax resist technique. Can you think of other subjects that could be used to combine line and color?

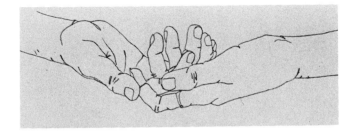

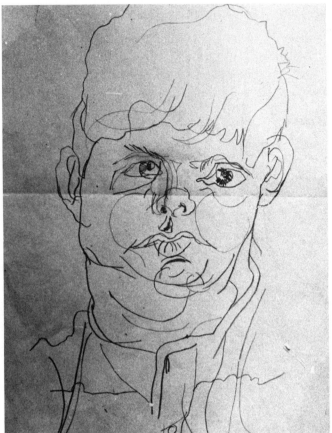

Contour drawing follows the edges and contours of a form. Look carefully and try to have your hand repeat what your eye sees.

Can you make crayon lines that express action, joy, anger, fear, strength, weakness? Can color create the expression? Can ink or pencil lines create the same feelings?

Hold a leaf or flower in your hand and draw it, using only line. Use pencil or pen and ink. Repeat the shapes and lines from various angles until you have many flowers or leaves. Let them overlap for a feeling of unity.

Other Suggestions

Bring a motor scooter or bicycle into the classroom. Make a contour drawing (outline only) of it using pencil, fibertipped pen or pen and ink.

Use multiple images—many line drawings—to express action. You might draw a bouncing ball or a tipping glass of milk. Can you show a bottle crashing or a bat hitting the ball? What other ideas might work in the same way?

Shape—Outline or Solid

Take a pair of scissors and cut several abstract *shapes* from sheets of construction paper. Can you cut people shapes? Or leaf shapes or flower shapes? If you had a pencil or a ball-point pen, could you draw the same shapes? Your drawings would be *outlines* of the shapes. Can you draw the shapes of a tree, car or pencil? Shapes themselves have no details at all.

If you place your cutout leaves on a sheet of black construction paper, you can see the shapes clearly. The cutout leaves are *positive shapes.* The shapes of the black background, between and around the leaves, are called *negative shapes.*

Some shapes have lines around them; others do not. Some shapes are colored. Other shapes are flat, textured or patterned. Can you draw shapes that are irregular, smooth, wiggly, leaf-shaped, geometric, free-form or jagged? How many other shapes can you draw? Can shapes be angry, quiet, fat, disjointed or symmetrical?

Use the side of a broken crayon or a sharp stick of charcoal. Quickly draw the shapes of students in active poses. Do not outline first. Simply try to sketch the *shape* of the models. Put several sketches on each sheet of paper, taking only a few minutes on each. You might also try to shade only the negative shapes around the models, leaving the figures white. You might try the same sketching techniques on fruit, trees, buildings or other shapes.

Cut the shapes of flowers, stars, people or other things from tagboard or heavy paper. You can also use abstract or geometric shapes. These can be used as stencils (both positive shapes and negative shapes). Use the sides of wax crayons to stencil color on paper and create a full page stencil drawing. You may use a single color or many colors. No line is needed.

Shapes can be solid or outlined. The solid shapes shown above were made with crayon, but no outlines were made first.

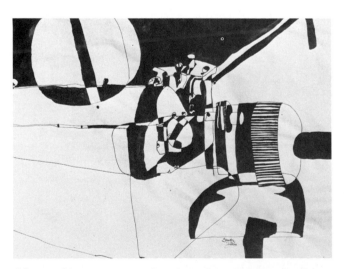

After making a contour drawing of part of a typewriter, this student filled in shapes with India ink and a wide pen point.

A

B

Crayon was used to draw silhouette shapes of student models. No outlines were drawn. The side of the crayon was used to capture the shape of the active pose (A). Crayon was also used (B) to fill in the negative space around the student models.

Shapes were cut from tagboard and used as stencils in this work. The student artist used crayon for the color. Can you tell how the stencils were used?

Other Suggestions

Use a brush and black ink to make the shapes of people, things or animals. Do not outline first. Use the brush to create the shapes. You might want to start with simple shapes, such as bottles, cans or teapots.

Look carefully at photographs that use black, gray and white to create shadows. Can you simplify these values into a drawing that uses no grays but only black and white shapes? This is a good way to learn how to simplify what you see.

Value and Form—Showing Three Dimensions

Darkness and lightness in drawing and painting are called *value*. The darkest value is black. What is the lightest value? There are an unlimited number of gray values between the extremes. These value changes and contrasts create a feeling of depth or shadow.

Abrupt or sharp value changes show sharp corners or edges. Gradual value changes show shadows on rounded forms. Can you use pencil values to shadow a cube and a cylinder? Use abrupt and gradual value changes to show forms.

Values can also be used to create moods in your drawing. Dark values give a somber and mysterious mood. What moods or feelings might be expressed with light values? Most drawings use contrasting values. It is easier to see the values on the surface of objects if you have only a single source of light. Shine a floodlight or a slide projector on your objects. This will emphasize the highlights (lightest values) and the shadows (darkest values). It will also help you to see the gradual or abrupt changes in values. Use this information in your drawings.

This linoleum block print was inspired by a black and white photograph. The gray values were taken out of the photograph so that only black and white shapes appeared. This simplified the subject. Then a drawing was made using pen, brush and ink. The linoleum cut was made from this drawing.

Pencils and charcoal show value changes best. Using pen and ink, find ways to use lines or dots to produce areas of gray.

Line up several simple still life objects. Use a single light source to emphasize the forms. Draw and shade with pencil.

Using pencil and paper, draw the outline of a single object. Then another drawing of the same object, using many values to show form.

Use charcoal to make a drawing of a student model. Sketch the outline lightly and simply. Then shade it with the charcoal, rubbing with a cloth to create smooth value changes. If colors or details make it hard for you to see the values, squint your eyes while looking at the subject. Notice the darkest and lightest places, and transfer that information to your drawing.

Other Suggestions

Make a geometric design with compass and ruler. Shade the shapes you have created with different values of pencil. You may also try pen and ink values, or wash drawing values.

Draw a face. Use yourself, another person, a sculpture or a mannequin as the model. Use charcoal or pencil to make values that will show the depth and roundness of the form.

Different concentrations of ink lines develop values and show forms. This student artist used only vertical lines to produce the needed value contrasts.

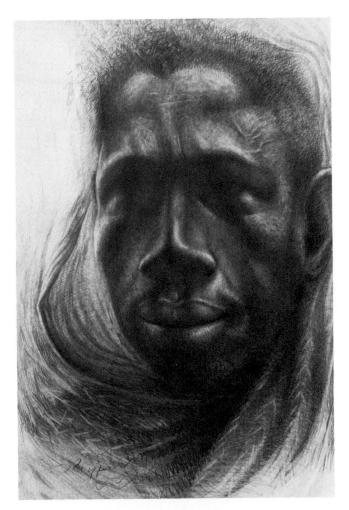

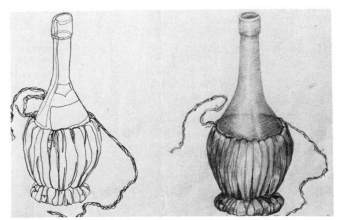

One bottle is drawn with contour lines. The other is shaded with pencil to show its form. You can make similar sets of drawings using a shoe, purse, basketball or eyeglasses.

John Biggers used charcoal to shade this portrait. It is more than three feet (91 cm) high. Can you see how light values and dark values show the form of the face? How did the artist show where the head bones are close to the skin?

117

Texture and Pattern—Adding Surface Interest

Rub your hand over your desk, your face or your clothes. What differences do you feel? How can you describe these *textures?* Rub your hand over several other surfaces and describe the feeling. Glass, tree trunks and book covers have different textures. To which of your senses do textures appeal?

Artists and photographers can make the surfaces of their work *appear* to be textural. This is called *simulated* texture. With a pencil or ball-point pen, see how many textures you can simulate on paper. Try dots, lines, slashes, circles or scribbles. You are creating a sense or feeling of texture where none actually exists. Do sculptors and weavers work with actual textures or simulated textures? You can cut examples of simulated textures from magazine photographs.

Patterns are repeated lines, colors or shapes in art. Often they create a feeling of texture. Plaids and tweeds are patterns. Ceiling and floor tiles create patterns. Can you find other patterns in the room around you? Pattern can be used to fill either positive or negative space in your drawings.

You can discover the surface texture of objects by making *rubbings* of them. Place a piece of bond paper or newsprint over an object and rub with the side of a crayon or pencil. Fill several sheets of paper with rubbings. Crayon rubbings can be washed with a contrasting color of watercolor to strengthen the textural feeling. Perhaps you can cut some of your crayon textures to create a fantasy monster or an imaginative bird or animal shape.

Draw the contour (outline) shapes of several figures from magazines. Overlap them when you transfer them to drawing paper. With pencil, fill in the spaces with patterns, simulated textures, words and doodles of your own design. A dark background will show the result best.

Several shapes of figures from newspaper ads were outlined and overlapped on drawing paper. The spaces were filled with pencil rubbings, lettering, signs and invented patterns.

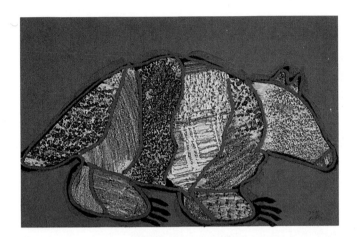

The flat sides of crayons can be rubbed over bond paper laid on textured surfaces. The rubbings then can be cut into shapes and combined to form imaginative animals. Yarn was added to outline and separate.

The student made contour drawings of still life items and then filled the shapes with dozens of patterns and textures using pen and ink. Patterns with larger and bolder lines develop contrast and interest.

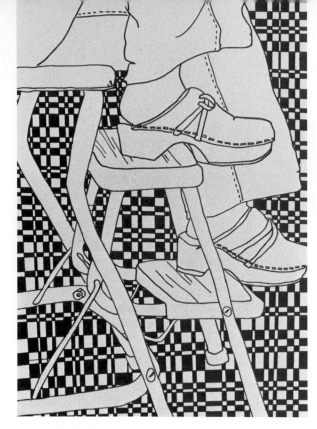

A pattern of inked squares fills the negative space in this drawing. This contrast emphasizes the contour-drawn forms.

Draw an outline of parts of mechanical devices (machinery or bicycle parts) or of furniture in the classroom. Use pen and ink to make different patterns in each area. Emphasize pattern rather than realism.

Other Suggestions

Use a ball-point or fibertipped pen and fill a page with simulated textures, such as sand, wood, stucco, or bricks.

Sketch a still life with pencil. Then use pen and ink textures to create the shading. Do not make your work too large, because it takes many fine lines to fill the page. Perhaps a gray wash over parts of the drawing will develop value contrast.

First this still life was drawn in pencil contour. Then the sheet was placed on textured surfaces and selected areas were rubbed with black crayon. Textured papers were added to create a collage. Finally, a heavy line of black tempera was added to unify the surface.

Space and Perspective—A Feeling of Depth

Drawing is done on a two-dimensional surface. Your drawing paper has only width and height. Boxes or apples have three-dimensions: width, height and depth. If you want to draw those objects so they *appear* three-dimensional, you must use techniques of *perspective drawing*.

1. *Overlapping.* If you make one object appear to be behind another, you create a feeling of depth.
2. *Shading.* If you can shade objects so that they seem to be rounded and casting shadows, they also appear three-dimensional.
3. *Placement.* If you are above a group of objects, the things closest to you should be drawn lower in the picture.
4. *Size.* If objects are the same size, the ones farther away will be smaller than the closer ones.
5. *Value.* Objects that are the same color appear to have lighter values as they get farther away from you.
6. *Focus.* Objects farther away are often fuzzy, while closer things have sharp edges.
7. *Linear perspective.* Parallel lines that lead directly away from you go to a single vanishing point. (Look at ceiling or floor tiles.) Lines that lead away from you at angles go to two vanishing points. You have worked with these ideas before. You may want to review them. You may want to draw boxes or houses in various perspective positions.

   Use several of these techniques to make drawings that emphasize depth and space. Draw people or still life objects. Use fruit or vegetable shapes, trees or abstract forms. Try *two or more* techniques in each drawing. Choose the drawing tools that will best express your idea on paper.

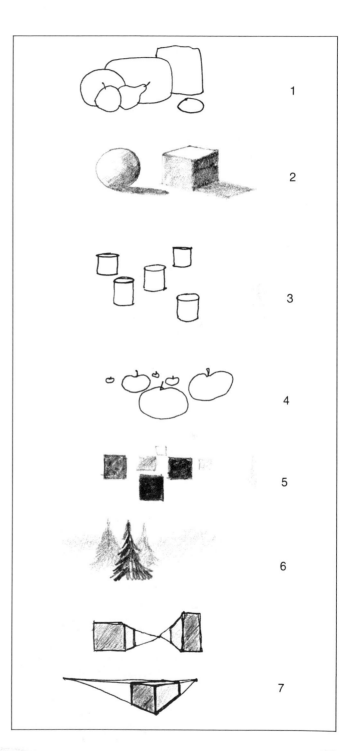

See how many perspective techniques there are in this complicated pencil drawing by Peter Paul Rubens, Abraham and Melchizedek. Collection of the Albertina Museum, Vienna, Austria.

A drawing exercise such as this one can help you understand two-point perspective and shading. Perhaps you can create an imaginary city on another planet, or unusual machinery.

Some Other Things to Try

As in other areas of art, drawing is going through an experimental period. Some artists are looking for new ways to use familiar tools. Others are trying new tools and ideas. Experiment to learn the limitations of some materials. This can open up exciting new ways to work.

Media can be mixed in different ways. Drawings can be made by scratching or washing materials *off* rather than putting them on paper.

Words, letters or numbers can be explored as possible drawing ideas. Try drawing on foil or plastic instead of paper. Use experimental tools such as cardboard, sticks, twigs, crumpled paper or plastic shapes to put ink on paper. You can draw on three-dimensional surfaces or make life-size portraits of yourself on cardboard.

Perhaps some of the ideas shown here will spark your interest in still other ways.

Artist Bob Peck put his family's Christmas greeting on a card that used letters and words to create both the message and the illustration.

7 Painting: Seeing Your World in Full Color

The artist in the studio takes a can of brown enamel paint and pours a blob on a sheet of Masonite. The panel is tilted to let the thick color run in long smooth streaks. The panel is laid flat to dry, and another one is started. After a day of drying, a second color is poured on the panels. Again they are tilted to produce more smooth streaks. The artist is making a painting but without using a brush. Not many artists work this way, but most have developed their own way of working.

Some painters use rulers and masking tape to get edges that are straight and crisp. Others brush paint on canvas in great juicy masses. Some thin the paint until it is transparent. Others spread it thickly with a knife. One artist might spray paint from a can or an airbrush. Another might apply color with bare hands.

Some painters use watercolor. Others use oils, enamels, acrylics, alkyds, lacquers, plastics or the ancient material of egg tempera. Today there are unlimited directions and many materials. Most artists experiment and develop new ways of working and expressing themselves.

All art communicates ideas. Painting seems to do it most completely. Through history, painting has been the most popular form of art. Egyptians and Greeks decorated their temples with brightly colored paintings. Romans painted people and scenes on the walls of their rooms. Early Christians used paintings to de-scribe religious events. During the Middle Ages, architecture, especially huge cathedrals, became the most important art form. But the Renaissance, which followed, burst forth with glorious color and painting. And ever since, painting has continued to be one of the strongest media for artistic expression.

Today's artists work in ways that are completely different from those of Renaissance painters. Even so, today's painters owe much to the great artists of the past. Since the beginnings of time, painters have recorded the joys and sorrows of the world. They have revealed inner thoughts. They have shown us real and imaginary landscapes. They have expressed loves and hatreds. They have painted religious works that were sometimes very personal. Painters have inspired revolutions, and have shown us peaceful gardens. They have explored color and light. They have given us a visual history of the world.

Styles of paintings range from realistic to abstract, with hundreds of variations in between. But regardless of style, artists are communicating their ideas and feelings. Painters can speak visually of love, hate, beauty, frustration or happiness. They can paint sorrow, faith, light or shape. They can describe people, patriotism, places, colors and things. They work in their own personal ways, telling their own special messages. Remember this when you begin your own paintings.

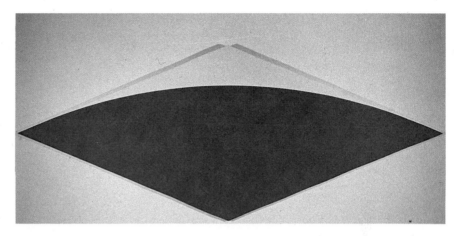

The Italian Renaissance painter, Raphael Sanzio, placed his Madonna and Child with Book *in a typical Italian landscape. The realism of the scene made the Biblical figures acceptable as real people. The 1504 oil painting is 22" × 16" (56 × 41 cm). Norton Simon Museum of Art, Pasadena.*

Janet Fish enjoys the challenge of painting the image of light passing through transparent, colored glass. Orange Bowl and Yellow Apple *is 46" × 50" (117 × 128 cm). Robert Miller Gallery, New York.*

Ellsworth Kelly is a hard-edge painter. He uses canvases of various shapes. This flattened diamond, 67" × 166" (170 × 436 cm) has a blue curved shape stretching across it. From some angles, Blue Curve III *(1972) looks like it is bending outward into space. Los Angeles County Museum of Art.*

125

Painting Materials, Tools and Techniques

Today artists work with many kinds of paint. Some are recent inventions. They have the traditional tools, and they have new types of brushes. They now have many unconventional painting tools, too. With today's variety of media, tools, and techniques, painting can be much more exciting than it was only a century ago.

The paint usually used in schools is called **tempera** or **poster paint.** It brushes easily and dries to a matte (dull) finish. It comes in liquid form, ready to use, or as a powder to mix with water. Water is all you need to thin the paint. It can become almost transparent. Water is all you need to clean brushes and work areas. You can add white paint to make **tints,** colors of lighter value. What would you add to make darker values? With tempera, you can paint over dried areas that have a different color. Don't scrub, or the colors will mix.

Transparent watercolor is another popular painting medium. In school, paint colors usually come in pans. These can be replaced when they are used up. The colors are transparent when mixed with water. When one color is brushed over another, both colors are visible. Do not scrub the colors or they will become muddy. No white paint is used in this medium. Lighter values are made by mixing more water with the paint. Actually, the white of the paper makes these thinned colors appear lighter in value. Thinned washes—mixtures of color and water—should be brushed on white or light paper, not over dark surfaces. Can you tell what would happen if washes were brushed over dark areas? Because watercolors are transparent, brush light colors on first. Add the darkest values last. If you need pure white in the painting, be careful to leave the paper unpainted.

Acrylic paints have a chemical base. They are soluble in water. After drying, however, they are much

Veloy Vigil's Silk and Beads *was painted in the vibrant and intense colors of acrylic paint. Painted on canvas, the 60" × 72" (152 × 182 cm) work shows how acrylics can look like they are full of light, even when the paint is brushed in an opaque and undiluted way.*

more permanent than tempera or watercolor. They can be applied thickly. You can thin them with water to make a transparent paint. You can apply them to any surface. You might try canvas, Masonite, paper, ceramics or glass.

Large paintings or murals (wall paintings) can be done with house paints, such as latex colors. These are water soluble, too. Like acrylics, they dry to a permanently hard finish.

Brushes are the traditional tool artists use to put paint on paper. Bristle brushes (stiff hairs) are best for tempera and acrylics. Soft brushes made of animal hair (squirrel or sable) are best for watercolor. They can also be used for detail and smooth work in tempera. Brushes made of synthetic materials are also suitable for most media. You may also paint with rollers, cardboard, painting knives, sponges, crumpled paper or even your fingers.

The surface on which you paint is called the *ground.* This is usually some type of paper. It can be textured or smooth, thin or thick, depending on your needs. Papers come with names such as oatmeal, bogus, drawing, charcoal, construction, bond, tagboard, folio board or newsprint. You should try some

This still life, painted by a student, shows the flat, opaque quality of the tempera paint used in most school artrooms.

Robert E. Wood made the soft edges of Golden East *by flowing watercolor over a wet surface. The crisp edges were painted on a completely dry surface. Can you see the transparency of the watercolor, compared to that of tempera?*

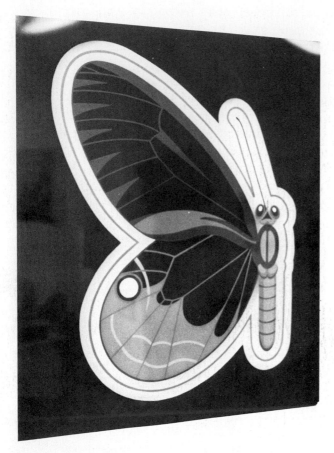

Rick Herold uses new materials to create his images. Here he uses Duco Auto Lacquer on a sheet of Plexiglas. Mystic Knight is painted on the back side of the surface, so that the bright, shiny colors reflect their surroundings. Orlando Gallery, Sherman Oaks, California.

of them to see what works best with different paints. You can also paint on canvas, Masonite, cardboard, pressed board or other surfaces. Most of these surfaces should be given a coat or two of white gesso or house paint before you begin to paint.

These are some of the materials you might use. Be on the lookout for new tools to try.

Techniques are the ways you handle your materials. What can you do with watercolor or tempera? How do you apply tempera to cardboard? Today experimentation with techniques is an important part of an artist's training. How can you combine crayon and watercolor? What painting tools can you use besides a brush?

Resist techniques can combine watercolor over rubber cement, white glue or crayon. Can you imagine the results in each case? The glue *resists* the paint. You may have tried some resist techniques already and want to experiment more.

Some colors can be *washed off* the surface after they have dried. After tempera colors have been applied and dried, cover the entire surface with India ink. When dry, hold the work under a faucet and wash off some of the paint. Stop when you like the effect, and let it dry.

Can you mix the resist and wash techniques to produce some exciting paintings? Try. Any technique that uses several different materials is called a *mixed-media* technique.

Perhaps you like to cut, tear and paste. You would enjoy creating a *collage.* This involves pasting materials—paper, fabric fibers—instead of painting. You can add some painting or drawing to your collage. This makes still another mixed-media technique. Can you think of several kinds of paper that might be useful in making collages? What glues would work for this kind of art?

You will usually work on paper or cardboard. You may also paint or create a collage on three-dimensional surfaces. Some artists place forms behind their paintings to make a bulge in the canvas. But you can make three-dimensional forms such as cardboard cones or cubes. Can you use paper pie plates or cups to help you? Could Styrofoam or paper forms be useful? You might coat some objects (such as shoes, bottles, boxes or jars) with white gesso, and then decorate them.

There is a range of painting experiences that you can enjoy, using common materials. Some projects are presented on the following pages. Collect painting ideas of your own that are interesting and exciting, and do some of them, too.

Patches of color were torn from magazines and used to create this collage. Paper was used instead of paint to produce a portrait of a classmate.

When brushing paint on paper, it is often easier to work standing up. Here the work is lying flat on the table, and the student brushes on color while standing over it.

How would you describe the mood or feeling in Scarecrow by Tyrus Wong. How has the artist created this mood? Notice how simply the subject matter is treated, and how effective it is. Is the painting transparent or opaque?

Crayon rubbings were used to pick up textures, and watercolor washes were brushed over to emphasize them. Black ink was then used to bring out underwater shapes and forms.

Some Design Suggestions

Do you remember how you started a drawing, by sketching the large shapes first? You should start a painting in the same way, lightly sketching major shapes. Often a few lines will be enough. Sometimes a few of the larger details can be sketched. Keep it simple.

If you are working with transparent watercolor, the lines you make will show through the color. They will become part of the paintings. Keep your lines light and simple or they will dominate the work.

Tempera and acrylics are opaque. If you use them, you will cover the sketch lines. They do not need to be detailed at all. You can add details as you paint, not in the first sketch.

All the elements of design are used in painting—line, value, color, texture, space, shape and form. Some people think color is the most important. Look back at the design section of this book and review the material on color. Do you know the three primary colors? When you mix any two of them, which secondary colors do they create? How do you get the in-termediate colors, such as red-orange? Do you remember what complementary colors are?

Artists may use colors to create moods in their works. Which colors might you use to show sadness or loneliness? Which would express happiness? Which colors are cool or warm? Which might be used for paintings of summer? Use these ideas to help you select your colors.

Painting uses the principles of design—balance, unity, contrast, pattern, emphasis, movement and rhythm. Look at any fine painting. Notice that the artist has considered these principles in the work. As you work on your own paintings, think about the arrangement of your subject matter. Position objects and color so that they reflect your knowledge of design. Ask yourself such questions as these: Are the colors in balance? Where is my center of interest? Does everything look like it belongs in the painting? Can I move some of the objects so that they lead my eye more easily to the center of interest?

Line is an important part of this watercolor. After the sketch was drawn and the watercolor added, heavy lines were brushed on with India ink. This unified the surface and emphasized the two main figures.

Pen and ink and watercolor washes were combined in this painting of a student's bedroom. A knowledge of perspective drawing is needed to work with this subject matter. Perhaps the painting suggests other subjects to you.

What Can I Paint?

Look around! There is subject matter for several dozen paintings in your classroom alone. The room, your classmates, a still life, the cleanup area, flowers, a corner, yourself, your hands, pencils or brushes, windows, light fixtures, bulletin boards, shelves of books, purses, shoes, faces, figures—all are part of your environment. Artists usually paint from their experiences and knowledge. All of these objects can find their way into your paintings.

If there are so many subjects in the room, think what can be found *outside* those four walls. You can paint scenes and objects around your school, hallways, gym classes, gardens, walks, trees, buildings, crowds. Look around you on the way home from school. Everything you see can be painted.

When you are home, look around for things to paint. The kitchen, living room, your room, the garage and the yard contain dozens of objects and scenes.

Think of your vacations. Search your memory for subjects. You can paint a swim in the ocean, a trip to the mountains, hikes, games, bicycle rides or cookouts.

Look closely at things around you, such as tree bark, peeling paint, the texture of rocks and concrete, the color of flowers. Notice the shape of leaves, the grain in wood or the polished reflection on glass. The more carefully you look, the more painting subjects you can find.

Set your imagination loose. Think about imaginary castles. Invent ugly monsters or cute animals. Imagine flying in space, landing on another planet, digging into the earth or winning great victories. Think about how to paint each of these.

Can you *say* something about your subject? Using an old favorite toy as subject, what can you tell about it? What colors might express your feelings of love and care? How can you show that it is discarded and old? How can textures show your feelings? What kind of background or setting will communicate your idea?

How do you *feel* about other subjects, such as football, dances, fishing, oil wells, slavery, sorrow, dressing up, winter holidays or animals? Can you express your feelings in painting?

Because every person's experiences and background are different, your paintings should also be different. Your personal work should reflect what you are, what you see and what you want to say.

Kevin Red Star paints the people around him. Because he knows his subjects so well, he can paint them in a very personal and unique way. Treasure State Gallery, Great Falls, Montana.

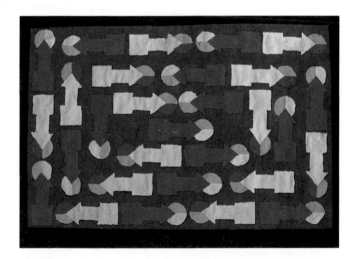

Simple shapes (arrow, circle) can be repeated to make an overall design in tempera paint. What other shapes and colors could be used to create different effects?

This student first sketched a pleasant memory from his summer vacation. Then, he painted it with acrylic paint and used a painting knife to catch the texture of the water and rocks.

Painting Still Lifes

Any arrangement of objects on a table can be called a still life. It can include bottles, fruit, cloth, boxes, toys or flowers. You can set up your own still life, or paint one that someone else arranged. You may wish to include every object in the still life or only paint a small part. You can make the colors realistic. You can paint with one color, plus black and white. You can even make a collage in parts. No matter how you work with it, it is always called a still life.

When you arrange your still life, try to include objects of various sizes, colors and textures. Why is this important? A draped cloth can be used as a background. You can also use colored paper or boards for backgrounds. You may even paint a background that you imagine. The still life may be in the corner of the room. It might also be placed in the center, with students working around it.

Set up a still life on a table and draw the large shapes first. Sketch the main shapes. Try to sketch their relationships correctly. Use watercolor or tempera to complete the painting. You may want to outline the objects or leave them alone. Watch for the highlights (lightest values) and the darkest values. Make your background (negative space) belong with the rest of the painting.

Use a simple still life setup, or a small part of a large arrangement. Fill the page with a pencil line drawing. Simplify the lines by drawing over them with a wide black line. Use tempera to finish the painting, allowing the new colors to partially cover the black lines. The lines should almost disappear in places. Add white to colors for highlight. What would you add to make the darker values? You may use a full range of colors or limit yourself to warm or cool colors.

Cut one or two objects from a magazine. Glue them on a large sheet of paper and paint a still life around them. You can invent the objects you add. You can use items from a still life in the room. Try to make the collage objects *belong* to the painting. Tempera paint will work well for this.

One of the wash-off techniques was used to produce this richly textured surface. Black crayon was added to outline the objects.

Part collage and part painting, this student still life bubbles with contemporary excitement.

Other Suggestions

Draw the simple shapes of a still life (real or imaginary) on heavy white drawing paper. Glue torn or cut pieces of bright, colored tissue paper to provide color. Try overlapping the colors to shade or to enrich the surface. You may also use magazine colors instead of tissue paper. Use white glue.

Use one of the resist techniques to create a still life with rich colors and textures.

Look at other still lifes in this book. They can provide you with ideas for paintings.

Brightly colored tissue paper was held to illustration board with clear lacquer. The student used a few ink lines to outline the shapes. Notice how overlapping colors produce rich combinations.

135

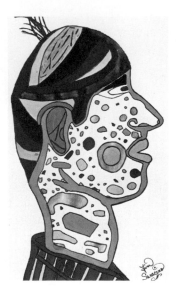

The Active World of People

Rembrandt painted portraits of friends and created many paintings of himself (self-portraits). Throughout history, most artists have painted people. Some subjects were imaginary. Others were famous. Some were kings and queens. Some were farmers and workers. Why are people the subject of so many paintings? Why are there fewer portrait painters today than 100 years ago?

Some paintings include the full figure of the person. Others are portraits, showing only the face and shoulders. Often artists capture the *character* of the person, as well as the features. Paintings of people might be realistic, abstract or a combination of both. Gather pictures from magazines that illustrate several types of portraits.

Often a painting of a person includes a definite environment. Some paintings show people at work. You might paint people playing soccer, having a pic-

nic or dancing at a party. It would *not* be important to show details of faces and figures. Instead, you want to capture the feeling or spirit of the event. People can also be shown as cartoon figures or silhouettes against a bright background.

If you are concerned with correct proportions, keep checking relative sizes of all of the features. How big are the hands compared to the face? How long is the upper arm compared to the lower arm? Where does the knee line up with the hip or ankle? Check these positions and sizes as you work.

Use any of the painting techniques to paint a student or teacher in a "working" position. Will you use tempera, watercolor, crayon resist or mixed media? Pose them with musical instruments, athletic gear, working tools, a bicycle or in other active poses.

Use classmates as models for portraits. Use bright colors to express a feeling about the person. You do not need to be realistic unless you want to.

Portraits give you the chance to express your feelings about people. Notice how many different styles were used by the students.

These two portrait paintings are very different. Pablo Picasso's Women with Book, 1932 *(left) shows us a redesigned figure sitting in a chair. He separated the parts of his model and put them back together in his own way. The high school artist painted her subject with great sensitivity. The model, sitting on the floor, is placed against a flat background that quietly emphasizes the figure. Picasso's work is from the Norton Simon Museum, Pasadena.*

Elaine de Kooning's portraits combine her sensitivity to personalities with extremely active brushwork. In this painting of Pele, *the world's premier soccer player, the artist used exploding color in the background to express Pele's dynamic athletic qualities.*

Other Suggestions

Cut some figures of people from magazines. Cut them apart and reassemble a collage of human forms. Perhaps the collage will be comical, perhaps not.

Lightly sketch the faces and partial figures of imaginary people in a group. Use a squeeze bottle of white glue to go over this simple outline. When it is dry, use pen and ink and watercolor washes to add pattern and color.

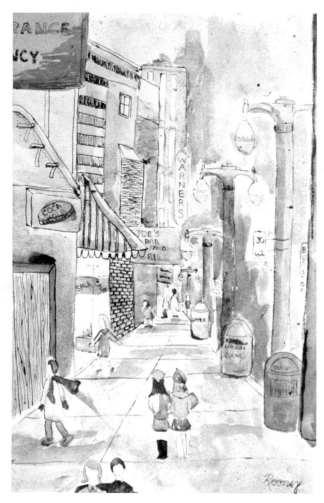

Various parts of the city were sketched on paper and painted in watercolor. Adding people, the student made the cityscape come alive.

Painting Your Environment

Whether you live in a large city, a small town or the country, you have subject matter for artwork. Your environment can include water, countryside, streets, walls, trees, flowers, buildings, signs, animals and people. You can paint any of these.

Paintings of your natural environment are called *landscapes.* Urban scenes are called *cityscapes.* What might be the subject matter in a *seascape?*

Think of your environment on a large scale. Think of your whole city or an entire mountain range. Now think of a single tree on your street, the rock garden in a neighbor's yard or your own back porch.

The colors of your landscape paintings can be realistic. Or you can imagine new colors. You may want to use warm colors to express your feelings about the desert. What colors might be used to express your feelings about a forest, a beach, a busy street or your room?

Some landscapes might also be imaginary. They might be illustrations for dream-like paintings or scenes from another planet. Landscapes can be realistic, abstract or designed. Your painted statements about places can be as personal as your portraits of people.

Use any of the painting techniques you have learned and create a landscape painting. Use your daily environment, or some place you remember, as your subject. Sketch lightly and use colors that suggest your feelings.

Use a street in your neighborhood as the subject for a tempera painting. Include the people, animals, signs, cars and colors that you typically see.

Other Suggestions

Go to a park, a farm or woods near your home or school. Sketch interesting scenes. Use these sketches as subjects for paintings. You may want to rearrange

These two paintings are of similar landscapes. It is easy to recognize the personal style of each artist, although neither painted the mountain subject in a realistic way. In Dong Kingman's watercolor (above left) of Yosemite in the Snow, 22" × 30" (56 × 76cm), the artist allows the white paper to represent snow. Notice his personal interpretation. Arthur Secunda used his collage technique in Lugano Suite #9, 40" × 30" (102 × 76 cm). He silkscreened his own colored papers and then tore, cut and glued them to create this stunning interpretation of a scene in the Italian Alps.

Geometric shapes—triangles, rectangles, squares and circles—are transformed into a cityscape. The rooftops of this imaginary city were done in watercolor and crayon.

139

some parts for your paintings. Sketch the simple large forms. Use watercolor or tempera to complete the painting.

Use a mixed-media technique to create an imaginary landscape. Perhaps a poem or a story in your literature book will give you ideas. Stretch your imagination. Think of new ways to paint landscapes.

Flowers and Plants

Impressionist painters, such as Auguste Renoir and Claude Monet, were very interested in painting landscapes. But winter weather would not allow them to paint in their favorite field or by the rivers. At these times, they would bring flowers into their studios and paint bouquets of colored blooms. The painters brought the outdoors inside.

Green plants make excellent subjects for paintings.

The branches and leaves of this plant were simplified by the student. Irregular white spaces were left between the color sections, creating a designed look to the watercolor.

Watercolor and ink were combined in this student's work. She concentrated on several leaves and a flower, painting to fill the sheet.

As with other subjects, you can make choices. You may paint flowers and plants realistically. You could use your own style and colors. You can create a collage for special effects. Use your imagination!

Paint flowers close up, as you hold them in your hands. Paint only a few and fill the page.

Use crayon resist techniques. Combine colored crayons and watercolor to paint a bouquet of bright flowers. You may want to work from live flowers. Artificial ones last longer for you to observe and paint.

Use your own style and colors to paint a close-up section of a living plant. Enlarge the leaves and branches in your artwork. Use tempera to color the painting.

Use tempera, watercolor, collage or a combination to paint many individual flowers. Cut and glue them to a backing to create a bouquet. Paint a vase (if you wish) and finish the background.

In Colleen Browning's oil painting, Danae No. 2, 48" × 45" (122 × 114 cm), the artist uses all the realistic colors of a tropical garden. The patterns of lush vegetation are seen in a dazzling light that intensifies their brilliant color. Kennedy Galleries, New York.

Other Suggestions

Make crayon rubbings of many textures on a large sheet of bond paper. Use watercolor washes to emphasize the textures. Use your imagination and allow these textures to suggest flowers and leaves. Use pen and ink or felt markers to outline imagined shapes and fill in the negative spaces. Add more crayon or watercolor to finish.

Tear colored tissue paper in flower shapes. Glue the shapes to a white backing board. Use white glue. Use bright colors for the petals and leaves. Glue complementary colors in the background. Many layers of colors will add depth and interest to your collage.

Painting Mechanical Objects

Bicycles, automobile engines, scales and the kitchen sink can provide subjects for paintings. Have you ever looked carefully at steam pipes, typewriters or ball-point pens?

Some paintings of mechanical objects might become Pop Art, depending on your style. To make Pop Art, enlarge small mechanical things such as watches, nail clippers, scissors or spark plugs. For other paintings you might use mechanical or manufactured objects in a still life.

Make a tempera painting of the fender of a car, with reflections. Paint an enlarged gear assembly from a ten-speed bicycle. Motorcycle engines and parts are excellent subjects. You can create paintings of the tools used in shop classes. You might include people, but your real subjects are the machines. No people are necessary.

Mechanical and manufactured objects are usually made from metal or plastic parts. They have hard surfaces. When you paint these objects, you can express this hardness with sharp, clean edges or lines. You may try to put the paint on paper with an even surface, to stress the mechanical quality.

Mechanical objects may allow you to work in a more abstract way. Or you may wish to become very precise and exact with your lines, edges and details. Your feelings will help you choose a direction.

Arrange mechanical parts in a small and simple still life. Include surfaces that are metallic. Create a tempera painting.

Arrange manufactured items from your kitchen. Sketch them first. Then outline them with pen and ink. Use transparent watercolor washes to add color. The ink lines should provide the quality of hardness.

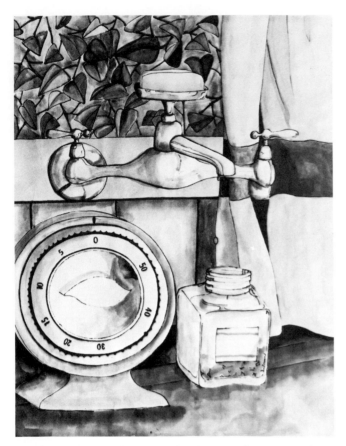

Mechanical items from your kitchen can be arranged to form a still life. Notice how this student used watercolor and ink lines to create a feeling of hardness.

Pen and ink, watercolor and collage were combined to create a Pop Art feeling. How have the parts of the painting been balanced?

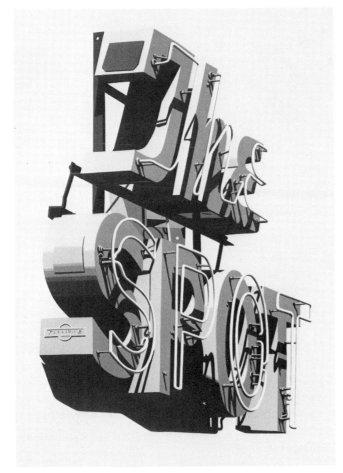

Robert Cottingham enjoys painting the shiny surfaces of metal and glass. In The Spot, 1978, *he explores the reflective surfaces of a huge, lighted sign. Careful observation is needed to see the value changes that create the forms. Done in acrylic on paper, the work is 23¼" × 15½" (59 × 40 cm).*

Other Suggestions

Use tempera and collage to make a design using pictures of mechanical objects. Select a theme for your material. You could gather fire trucks, steam trains, automobiles or carpenter's tools. You could make groups of giant machines or tiny tools.

You can make an assemblage of mechanical or manufactured items. Glue them on a Masonite panel. Use tempera or acrylic paint to fill in the negative space and unify the composition.

Can you think of ways to create paintings of automobiles, farm machinery or earth-moving equipment? Can you depict a small part of the subject instead of the entire thing? Perhaps a field trip to an equipment yard will provide sketches for your paintings. If you live near water, can ships or boats serve as subjects?

The more active the subject, the better for LeRoy Neiman. He used painting knives and brushes to catch the excitement of the first Ali-Foreman fight. Can you see how this style is perfectly suited to his subject matter?

The Whirl of Action

Running, flying, bouncing, fighting, sailing, walking, climbing and *slashing* all bring pictures of action to your mind. Can you think of other action words?

Artists have ways to express action, too. Edges can be blurred, as in photographs of action. Lines can be slanted. Clashing colors may create a feeling of action. Swirling eye movement and strong value contrasts help show action. Sketchy or incomplete paintings give the feeling that even the artist was hurrying.

Some artists express action by using great slashes of color. Their painting style, *Asbtract Expressionism,* is sometimes called *Action Painting.*

Sports are active, but athletes are difficult to sketch because they move so much. What can help you see just how athletes move and bend in motion? Which sports might show the most active people?

Animals are active. So are boats, automobiles, motorcycles and waving flags. Can you think of other active things?

Use photographs of active athletes for an outline or silhouette. Place this outline form on one side of your paper. It is best to have the action moving *into* the center of the page. Draw lines around the figure to show expanding spaces that are thinner in some places than in others (see the example). Start with the figure and paint the spaces gradually darker as you move to the outside. You may also start with a pure color (yellow) at the figure, and add a bit of its complementary color (violet) as you move outward. Try to keep the edges as smooth as possible. Vibrations help express action in the painting.

Sketch several figures at play or in a game. Try to paint them with rapid brushstrokes and very little de-

A student photograph of a pillow fight provided the model for this acrylic painting. Notice how edges are blurred to show action. Dry-brush marks, in large swirls, give the feeling of action.

The basic shape of a runner is surrounded by radiating color that produces a visual vibration. Each ring of the tempera color has a little more black added to it as it goes outward.

tail. Have your brushstrokes emphasize the direction of the action.

Experiment with *drybrush* techniques. Have your brush partly dry and drag it across the surface of the painting.

Other Suggestions

Paint a race car, speedboat or airplane. Paint it so that you stress speed and action. Think of techniques before you begin.

Use a large brush and tempera, watercolor or a combination. Create an abstract painting that says *action.* Do not use recognizable objects in this painting. Let the paint and brush *show* the action.

Use watercolor to paint the action of a storm at sea or on the coast. Can you use tools other than brushes? Can fingers and sponges be called painting tools?

Just Imagine That You . . .

Just imagine that you were a thousand feet down in the ocean, or able to fly over streets and farmland. How would things look? Use your imagination to see strange places and peculiar animals. Perhaps you can imagine the most beautiful spot in the world. Use various painting techniques to show your friends what you can imagine.

Can you invent new designs for playing cards or create a new automobile? You can make a design based on an astrological sign or a religious symbol. You may get more ideas as you begin to research your subject.

Can you imagine a decorative sunburst or a marvelous new flower? You might design a stained glass window, using colored tissue paper and black construction paper or black tempera. Can you imagine a breathtaking castle or the most ugly creature in the universe? Can you combine a beetle shape with some mechanical monster?

Let your imagination go. Write a list of fantastic places, things, animals or inventions. Use any of the techniques you know, and materials you have, to paint or create a collage of your idea. Choose materials that will best help you express your idea. Combinations of materials often work well with these ideas.

A few torn shapes suggest a complete landscape. Arthur Secunda made Big Black Sur, *(above), 1983, in black and white. It is 30" × 22" (76 × 56 cm).*

You can combine collage, drawing and painting to create an imaginative happening.

Lee Krasner used active brushstrokes to express the feeling of Celebration, 1980. She did not have to paint any people to create the feeling of a party. The oil painting is 92" × 184" (234 × 468 cm). Robert Miller Gallery, New York.

To make this abstract painting, a student isolated an eye from a portrait photograph, simplified it to only two values, and painted it with two flat colors.

Carla Pagliaro covered a canvas with acrylic paint, crumpled it into a three-dimensional form and combined it with wood. She created a unique sculptural painting.

Experimenting with Materials and Ideas

In an age when experimentation is an important part of the art scene, you may wish to work in several different ways. You might try some new painting materials. You could make your own. You can work on different surfaces, even three-dimensional ones.

You can experiment with abstract shapes or textures. You may like to experiment with combinations of materials, or add actual objects to a painting. Your experiments may be based on your organization of space on your page.

You can go in several directions. Perhaps the examples on these pages will get you started. But they may be only the beginning of your ideas. Enjoy working in experimental ways. Try to keep the principles of design in mind.

8 Printmaking: Many Images of a Single Idea

The Dutch painter Rembrandt liked to spend his evenings scratching designs on a copper plate by candlelight. Does this surprise you? The artist was really most noted for his paintings. He could not paint at night, though. Candlelight was too dim.

So Rembrandt spent evenings working at his favorite printmaking technique—etching in copper. When his metal plate was ready, he could make prints. He could pull many prints from one copper plate. Rembrandt would sign them all. All of them are original prints, made by the artist.

A printmaker can create many images that are almost exactly alike. The artist is involved with the entire process, so each copy is considered a signed, original work.

The need to produce prints was economic. Great artists, such as Albrecht Dürer and Rembrandt, could demand high prices for their paintings. But original prints, because there were many images, could sell for less money. And during the late Renaissance (sixteenth century) this was an important consideration. It allowed more people to own the works of great artists. And artists gained a broader audience.

Today printmaking is a major art form. Many important artists are involved in printmaking. Large exhibits of prints are often seen in major museums and galleries.

Many artists work full time at some kind of printmaking. Today printmaking is one of the most experimental and exciting areas of art. New materials and processes have given artists new avenues of expression.

An artist producing one hundred prints can have his single image on view in one hundred locations. A single painting can be shown in only one place at a time. Many artists have begun making prints because they wish to have wider audiences.

Basic Printmaking Techniques

There are four basic printmaking techniques used today. Although artists may experiment and produce new variations, the basic techniques still are these four. The accompanying diagrams will help you understand what happens in each technique.

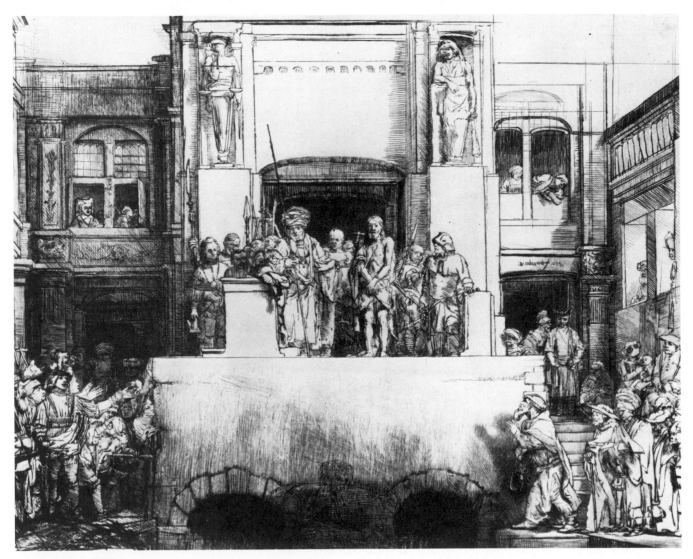

Thousands of fine lines were cut into the copper plate as Rembrandt worked on Christ Presented to the People. Can you see how he used lines to produce different values? How did he show the lightest values? Collection, Los Angeles County Museum of Art (The Mr. and Mrs. Allan C. Balch Fund).

Relief Prints

You are probably familiar with relief prints, such as woodcuts and linoleum cuts. Your fingerprint is a relief print. So are potato prints. In relief printing the raised surface is inked with a brayer and printed (Diagram A).

Wood or linoleum can be cut with a knife or a gouge. The artist removes *unwanted* areas or lines. These cutout parts will be white in the print. What is left (the raised surface) will print the ink. Pressure is needed to transfer ink from the block to the paper. Pressure can be applied with a spoon, your hand or a press.

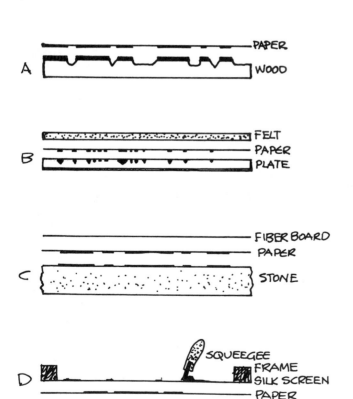

Contemporary printmakers combine many techniques. Richard Wiegmann, in Just About the Most Wonderful . . . , *uses intaglio (etching), blind embossing (no ink used), silk-screen, silver mylar and paper.*

Etchings

The printmaker draws lines on a plate. Usually the plate is made of metal or plastic. If the artist scratches the plate to make lines, it is called *drypoint etching.* If the artist uses acid to create lines in the plate, it is called an *etching.* If the lines are gouged out, it is called an *engraving.* But in all these processes, the lines do the printing (see Diagram B).

Ink is rubbed *down into* the cutout lines, and the surface of the plate is wiped clean. When great pressure is applied with a press, the dampened paper is forced into the lines where it picks up the ink. So it is the removed area and not the raised surface that does the printing.

Lithographs

It is easy to draw with a greasy crayon or ink on a smooth limestone block or metal plate. That is how an image is prepared on a lithographic stone. This printing method is more difficult than any other printmaking process.

Lithographs are possible because water and grease do not mix. First, the artist creates a greasy drawing on the stone. Then the artist cleans the surface with an acid. Water is sponged on the surface. Of course, it runs off the greasy drawing and wets only the stone (or metal). Next, greasy ink is rolled on with a large leather roller. The water on the stone resists the ink. The ink is attracted easily to the greasy drawing. The artist places paper on the surface. Stone and paper are run through a large press (Diagram C).

In this process, no cuts are made in the stone's surface. The print is made by transferring ink from the greasy drawing to the paper.

Silk-Screen Prints

The newest method of printmaking is the silk-screen print, or *serigraph.* No cutting or rolling is necessary. Many colors can be used.

Silk is stretched on a wood frame. The colored ink is forced *through* the silk with a rubber squeegee (Diagram D). The image is made by a stencil. The stencil may be made of paper or a brushed-on substance. The stencil blocks out the ink in some places. This produces the design on the paper underneath. Look through the silk-screen section of this book for details and examples.

The process of lithography is illustrated in this work by Henri de Toulouse-Lautrec. L'Estampe Originale is a multicolored print, in flat colors, outlined with a dark line. The Metropolitan Museum of Art, Rogers Fund.

Design Suggestions

In all printmaking techniques, you must first prepare the printing surface or screen. The quality of the finished print depends on the quality of the printing surface, so prepare carefully. Your attention to details and your technique can produce good prints.

Decide what image you will create. Then choose a printmaking technique that will help say what you want. Which method will create the best print of an elephant? Prints of storms, crashing waves or delicate flowers might call for different techniques. Woodcuts are good for bold statements. Etchings are best when fine lines are desired. Silk-screens can be used if you want to work with several colors.

Turn back to the design section to review the elements and principles of design. Use this information in your printmaking. You can add interest by using a variety of lines, shapes, values, textures and colors. Just as in painting or sculpture, use the principles of balance, unity, movement, emphasis, contrast and pattern. These will help you arrange your art work effectively.

Relief Printmaking—A Review

You have probably made a linoleum print or a potato print. If not, or if you enjoyed the process, you might make one before going on to other printmaking activities.

Examples of various relief prints are shown here. Perhaps you can cut some large blocks or print several small blocks together to make a large print. You can use string to create string prints. This is another way to create a relief surface. You might use textile ink to print on fabrics. Is there a place in school or at home where handprinted fabrics could be used? You

You may combine several of your blocks in a single print. This student used two linoleum prints and some brayer printing.

could plan a group print project as a gift for a children's hospital or a nursing home.

Some artists spend all their lives using one printmaking technique. You might prefer to use your favorite printmaking technique. Or you might like to try some of the techniques that follow.

Some of the processes require a lot of equipment. Not all schools can use every technique. Be sure that you have the equipment you will need.

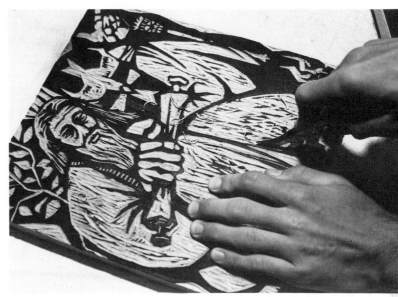

In relief printmaking, the areas cut away by the gouge remain white. The raised areas receive ink and print on paper.

A class printmaking project might be to make a set of alphabet picture cards that can be given to children's hospitals or nursery schools.

DECK OF
alphabet picture cards

James McNeill Whistler was one of America's best-known etchers. Black Lion Wharf *combines loose drawing in the foreground with precise detail in the buildings of the background. All of this is done with line. The Metropolitan Museum of Art (Harris Brisbane Dick Fund).*

Drypoint Etching—the Line Does the Printing

The etching process is also known as the intaglio technique, pronounced "in-TALL-yo." The surface of the metal plate has lines cut into it. These may be created by scratching (drypoint), with acid (etching), or by gouging (engraving). Ink is forced *into* the cut lines and the surface is wiped clean. Dampened paper is forced into the lines with great pressure from the press. The ink is transferred to the paper from the cuts.

Fine lines and careful detail are characteristic of the etched plate. Images can include shading created with dots or cross-hatching. Fine lines are the special beauty of this printmaking medium.

Etchings became important in the sixteenth century. They were elaborate and detailed. Martin Schongauer was the first to create fine etchings. Albrecht Dürer and Rembrandt were painters who became very skillful at creating etchings.

Most often the intaglio process involves acids and expensive tools to cut a metal plate. You can do one part of the process if your art room has a roller printing press. Drypoint etchings are created by scratching thin lines into the printing plate. This is followed by inking and printing.

What subject matter might work well when fine lines are used? What other techniques make use of very fine lines?

Draw your subject matter (perhaps insects or plants) with a ball-point pen. Use a sheet of paper that is no larger than your press bed. Your print will be a mirror-image of your drawing. Plan ahead!

Place your reverse drawing under a piece of heavy acetate or celluloid. The acetate or celluloid will be your printing plate. Scratch lines into the plate with a compass point or another sharp tool, held vertically. The scratches should be deep enough to feel when your finger is run over the surface. Check on the progress of your scratched design by sliding a piece of dark construction paper under the acetate.

Etchings must be printed on dampened paper. This is because the paper must be forced *into* the scratches. Use heavy drawing paper that is a little larger than your printing plate. Soak the drawing paper on both sides under a faucet or in a tub of water. Stack it between two large blotters or other absorbent paper to remove extra water.

Ink the plate with dark or earth-colored oil paint or printing ink. Burnt umber, burnt siena or black work best. Rub it into the scratches with a cloth, a felt dabber or a strong paper towel. Carefully wipe the

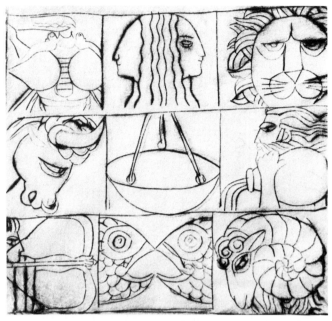

Zodiac symbols were printed in drypoint. Notice the simplicity of the line work. Etchings produce mirror images just as relief prints do.

Simple lines can be very effective in drypoint etchings. These lines were scratched into an acetate sheet that was placed over the original drawing.

155

Structures with line construction make excellent subjects for drypoint etchings. This print is approximately 10" (25 cm) high.

The tone of the sky was created by wiping the plate, leaving some ink on the surface. After you have done a few prints, you'll get a feeling for how much ink to leave on the plate.

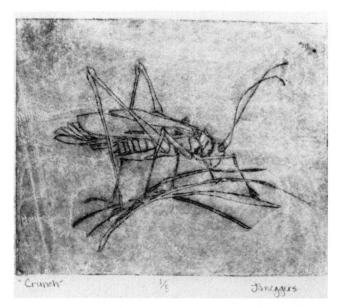

"Crunch"   ⅕   J.niggers

Bugs and insects make excellent subjects for drypoint etchings scratched in plastic. This one is 6" (15 cm) wide, with simple but effective line work.

surface with a newspaper scrap or tarlatan cloth. Do not wipe the ink out of the lines. It is alright to leave a little ink on the unscratched acetate. This will give a tone to the print.

Place the inked plate face up on the bed of the press. Lay your dampened paper over the plate. Place two sheets of felt over the paper and run it all through the press. The heavy pressure will force the paper into your scratched lines. The paper will suck out the ink and transfer the design to the paper.

Hang the prints up to dry, or tack or tape them to a drying board.

Use paint thinner to clean up oil paints and ink. **Do not leave thinner on your skin. Do not breathe fumes. Follow all other safety precautions.** The plates need not be cleaned. They can be left ready for more printing.

Other Suggestions

In etching, shaded areas can be produced by cross-hatching or stippling with dots. Are there other ways to allow the print to take on the feeling of dark shading?

Use masking tape to hold your materials (the drawing and the acetate plate) as you scratch in the plate.

When dry, trim the prints, but leave an inch or so of paper around the edge. Lay the prints under a stack of books or another large weight to flatten them. Sign them in pencil *under* the lower right corner of the print, not in the print itself.

If no printing press is available, you can press with a spoon back to transfer the print. But because much pressure is needed, the acetate will buckle after a few prints. It might even tear. It will probably be usable for only a few prints.

Ink left on the acetate provides a background tone for the line work. It also can be controlled to produce a shading effect.

The pressure of two felt pads is usually needed to make a good print of an etching. The pressure forces the paper into the scratched lines where it absorbs the ink.

Silk-Screen Printing—Serigraphy

Many vivid colors, smooth flat shapes, crisp edges—all these are part of silk-screening. This is an exciting twentieth-century addition to the world of printmaking. Colored ink is forced *through* a stencil onto the paper below the silk-screen, and a print is produced. The process can become quite complicated in the hands of a professional printmaker or a commercial designer. But there are some simple ways to produce serigraphs (silk-screen prints).

Bottle labels, posters, advertisements on buses, greeting cards, wrapping paper and large photo murals all can be silk-screened by commercial artists. Fine art printmakers use the same techniques to create prints for framing.

The basic tools are a frame with silk stretched across it (see the diagram and its explanation), stencils and a rubber squeegee.

Stencils can be produced in many ways. We will explore only one method of blocking out the ink from the print. Others are listed in the following pages, in case you wish to experiment further.

The *paper stencil* method involves cutting or tearing paper (bond paper, waxpaper or newsprint) to produce the stencil. What sorts of edges can you make by cutting or tearing? How can you produce lines with this technique? What subject matter will work with such flat shapes of color? Will abstract or geometric shapes work well?

Cut a design, shape or lines out of the center of a sheet of paper. This is your first stencil. It should be taped with masking tape to the **bottom** of the screen frame. If the paper doesn't cover the opening in the frame, use other paper or paper tape to fill in around the edges. This will prevent stray ink from getting on the print.

Simple shapes are easy to print. Two colors were used here, with a separate stencil for each. Spaces were cut from the center of a piece of paper and ink passed through them to make the print.

A. *Printing frame of 2" x 2" pine, about 2 or 3" larger in all directions than the design.*

B. *Silk stretched taut on frame and stapled in place on the bottom of the screen frame. (Organdy or nylon may also be used.)*

C. *Baseboard (¾" plywood or an old drawing board), several inches larger than the printing frame.*

D. *Two slip-pin hinges to keep frame in place. Pins must be removable so screen can be cleaned at the sink.*

E. *The squeegee is a rubber blade held in a wooden handle used to force ink through the silk. It must be long enough to cover the design to be printed in one pull across the screen.*

F. *Kick leg that is loose and can hold frame in open position.*

G. *Paper or cloth to be printed, under the screen.*

H. *Registration tabs that insure getting the paper back in the right place for a second printing.*

Paper stencils may be folded and cut with scissors. The design also may be cut with a stencil knife. Stencils can be torn, punched or cut from a flat sheet of paper. Ink passes through the open areas of the stencil to the paper below.

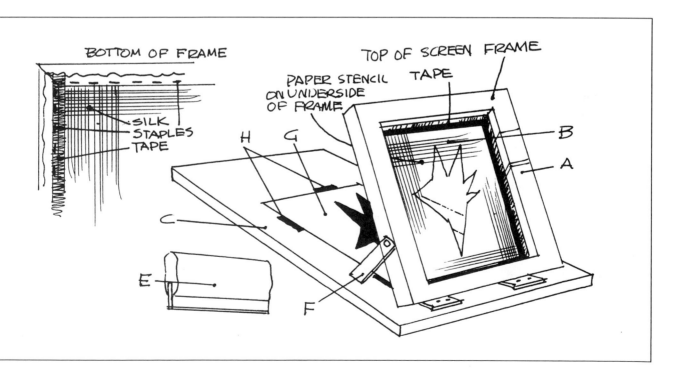

BOTTOM OF FRAME

TOP OF SCREEN FRAME

TAPE

PAPER STENCIL ON UNDERSIDE OF FRAME

SILK
STAPLES
TAPE

H G

C

E

F

B

A

Two paper stencils were all this student needed to create a city at sunrise.

Tambourines inspired this multicolored serigraph. It was made with paper-cut stencils.

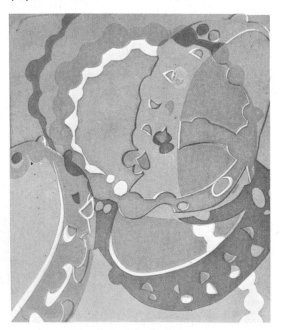

If you use the cutout shapes as part of the design, you cannot tape them to the screen. Simply lay them in place *under* the screen. When the first ink is pulled across the screen, the shapes will stick in the proper place. Tiny shapes can be stuck to the underside of the screen by gluing with library paste or some other glue. Do *not* use a permanent glue, such as Wilhold or Elmers.

Lower the frame after releasing the kick leg. Spoon the ink (water-soluble screen ink) across the edge of the screen, near the hinges. Hold the squeegee in both hands, slanted slightly toward you. *Pull* it toward you all the way across the screen. This forces the ink down through the screen. Lift the squeegee and slant it away from you. Then *push* it back to the top of the frame. Use enough pressure to clean the ink off of the screen.

Lay the squeegee on the top of the frame. Raise the frame slowly. Set the kick leg again and remove your print. Insert another piece of paper, lower the frame and make the next print.

Hang the prints to dry or place them on a drying rack. If there is room, simply spread them on a table.

When the printing is finished, remove the ink from the frame with a plastic or cardboard card. Return the ink to the bottle or can. Now remove the slip pins from the hinges, take off the stencil and wash the remaining ink from the silk. Clean the screen immediately and carefully. Dried ink will act just like another stencil. It will block out color from your later prints.

Other Suggestions

If your brand of printing ink includes a material to slow the drying time, use it to extend your printing time and ease cleanup.

Letters or numbers will *not* be reversed as in other printing methods.

Several colors may be used in one print by printing a second stencil over the first one, after it has dried.

Place a second stencil (or cutout paper) in place on the silk and print with another color. Get all the prints in the correct position using three registration tabs or bits of masking tape at the edges of the paper (see the diagram).

There are some commercial screen fillers that can be painted on the top of the screen with a brush. When dry, they act like a stencil. Be sure you know what solvents will clean out each kind of filler. Always remove the ink and clean up completely before removing filler from the screen. Use all safety precautions.

You can make colors transparent by adding commercially prepared extenders to your printing ink. Can you think of uses for transparent colors in silk-screen prints?

Finished prints should be trimmed, leaving about an inch of paper around each one. Sign them *under* the print, at the lower right corner.

Photographs can be silk-screened using commercially prepared materials. Check with companies that might help you with this process.

You can get a very different effect if you draw on the silk with a wax crayon. Press firmly. Draw your lines on the top of the silk. Use only water-based inks to print this image. Oil-based inks will dissolve the crayon. The edges of the finished print will be soft and crayonlike. Use this technique in combination with another technique. When the printing is done, use paint thinner or lacquer thinner to clean the crayon from the screen. **Do not leave thinner on skin. Do not breath fumes. Follow all other safety precautions.**

The squeegee is slanted slightly toward you to pull the ink across the screen. Reverse the slant to push the squeegee back to the top of the screen frame.

The color of the paper provided the background for this three-color print. The simplified stencil has an excellent sense of action and design.

Pressed leaves and flowers are combined with string, sand and glue in this student collagraph. The textured background is controlled by the wiping process.

Cut tagboard, string, paper and glue were used to make the plate for this print.

This collagraph plate has been inked and then wiped off in places to control values. It is now ready to print. Sand, string and tagboard were glued to the cardboard plate before it was inked.

Collagraphs—Combination Printing

Relief prints transfer their images from raised surfaces. Intaglio prints transfer their images from below the block's surface. *Collagraph prints* combine these two. If you have a roller printing press, you might try experimenting with this exciting printmaking medium.

Use heavy folio board or thin Masonite for the basic plate. This should be smaller than the bed of your press. On the surface of the plate, you can glue various textured objects. Try using thin cardboard, paper, leaves, various tapes, paper or plastic lace, textiles, or anything else that is flat and will create interesting surface textures. Try adding PVA glue in drips and trails. Sprinkle sand on some glued places. Arrange the items to produce an interesting design. When all is dry, seal the entire surface with acrylic medium, acrylic gesso or shellac. Acrylic gesso can also be used instead of glue.

You can ink the plate with oil paint. Use earth colors for the best results (burnt siena, raw umber, burnt umber, brown or black). Rub the paint into the surface with a wadded cloth, felt dabber or bristle brush. Cover the surface and rub down into all the cracks and textures. Wipe off the extra color with a paper towel or squares of newspaper. Experiment until you know about how much to wipe off.

Dampened paper—heavy drawing paper, soaked or wet on both sides—should be laid over the inked plate. This paper should be a bit larger than the plate. Lay two felt sheets over the paper. Run the entire sandwich through the press. Great pressure is needed to force the paper into the surface textures to pick up the ink.

Trim your prints and sign them under the lower right corner.

Collagraph printmaking can be very exciting. Clare Romano created *Dusk Canyon* by segmenting the plate into four pieces. These were collaged, textured, inked and reassembled before printing. She used six colors of ink to make this print.

Other Suggestions

You can run simple collagraphs through the press without inking the plate. Use dampened paper, so it records the textures of the plate. This process is called *blind embossing,* and it will show only the textures of the plate and no color.

After printing, the ink-stained collagraph plates make excellent pieces of art themselves. Save them.

You might ink and print string prints as collagraphs for a different effect. Experiment.

Experimental Prints and Other Ideas

Printmaking includes many techniques and varieties. It can be used for many experimental activities. Often printmakers use techniques that they have developed through years of work and many experiments.

Try combining several printmaking techniques in one print. Can you silk-screen over a woodcut? Try a block print over a discarded silk-screen background. Or print a collagraph over an old linoleum print. Use some of your old or discarded prints as backgrounds for something new. Experimentation can lead to new techniques.

Print a variety of found objects on colored construction paper. Use tempera paint as the printing ink.

Use a soft rubber brayer to ink your collagraph plate with block printing ink. Use this method instead of the regular collagraph inking process. Use a press or spoon to transfer the color to paper. Notice how different the print is when compared to your original collagraph.

Use liquids that harden when dry, such as gesso, acrylic modeling paste, Sculptmetal or other liquid metals. Coat a cardboard or Masonite plate. Press some items into it, such as coins, medals or textured fabric. Allow the material to harden. (Put a coating of oil on the objects before you press them in. This will help you release them after drying.) Ink this surface with a cloth and oil paint, and treat it as a collagraph. Try using this technique in making regular collagraph plates. Can you make other marks in the material as it is drying? Use a brayer to ink these plates, and notice the different result.

Using a soft rubber brayer, ink and print all sorts of found objects, such as crushed tin cans, crumpled paper, plastic doilies, manufactured metal parts or bottles. Can you combine this technique with collagraphs or serigraphs?

These ideas may lead you to invent several techniques or combination prints of your own. That is how new printmaking methods are discovered—through experimentation. After you are familiar with the basic techniques, experiment on your own.

Always print ten copies or more of each image. After they are signed, you may wish to trade prints with your classmates. In this way you can begin your own art collection.

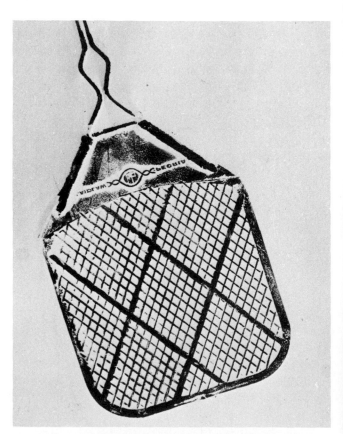

Flat plastic things, such as this flyswatter, can be inked and printed. Can you find more items like this to print? Use your hand to press down on the paper when printing.

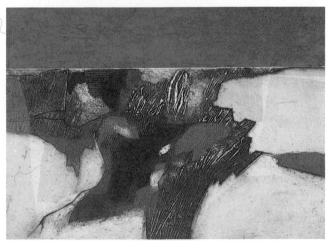

Try illustrating a line from a poem. This illustration is a linoleum cut. The letters and words are cardboard prints.

The letters and numbers on this student calendar were cut from linoleum and glued to wooden spools for printing. The illustrations for each month were silk-screened in various colors from paper-cut stencils.

Clare Romano experiments with textured printing surfaces. Her *Night Canyon* collagraph is printed in four colors from two separate plates. One was cut in half and reassembled for printing. The large work is 22" × 30" (56 × 76 cm).

9 Sculpture: Creating in Three Dimensions

One artist has permission to use a plastic-forming machine owned by his company. But instead of using the firm's steel molds to produce thousands of look-alike plastic parts, the sculptor lets the machine ooze globs of liquid plastic on a board. While the material is still workable, the artist pokes, pulls and stretches the plastic to create fantasy shapes. This sculptor is creating three-dimensional forms (sculptures), but not in any traditional way.

The earliest sculptors carved wood and stone. Often they created images of their gods. Other times they decorated their tools or weapons with carved forms. Often they simply produced handsome carved decorations.

Artists modeled clay many centuries ago, too. They made ceramic or terra-cotta figures of people, gods and animals. Sometimes these figures were glazed. Often they were simply fired and rubbed to get a finished effect.

Later people learned to melt metals and pour them into molds. Artists used this casting technique to create sculptures of bronze, gold, lead or silver.

Until recent times, carving, casting and modeling were the only ways to form sculptures. Today there are new techniques of *construction,* such as nailing, tying, gluing or welding. Now sculptors have fewer limits on the way they can work. They can use many methods available to produce three-dimensional forms.

Sculpture materials have also taken on a new look in recent years. Formerly artists carved wood and

The Indians of western Mexico were creating terra-cotta sculptures before Columbus landed in the Western hemisphere. Figures such as this one are concepts of human forms rather than exact likenesses. Collection of Mr. and Mrs. Joseph Gatto, Los Angeles.

stone. They poured hot metals into molds, or they modeled clay. Today's sculptors use a broader range of materials. Some use plastic, electricity, sound or water. Others use epoxies, resins, fiber glass or brass. Still others may use glass, laser beams, old metal parts, fluorescent tubes or fibers.

With new materials and technology, sculpture has become a fascinating way to express ideas. Electricity can make sculpture come alive with movement. Hydraulic systems produce large and complex action in sculptures. Padding and sewing can be used for soft sculptures. Sound and moving lights can produce life and action. Some of today's sculptors still work in the traditional ways. Many others are looking for new materials and new directions to express the spirit of the twentieth century.

Some sculptures are huge (the Statue of Liberty) while others are very small (a wooden dog for your desk). This chapter shows you a variety of materials, sizes and subjects. Think about what kinds of sculptures you will create.

Gianlorenzo Bernini's David *is a life-size sculpture carved from a single marble block. The work, made in 1623, shows David as a twisting form, ready to unleash a slingshot at Goliath. Notice how John Chamberlain's work (right) repeats, in an abstract way, the visual movement of Bernini's active form.*

John Chamberlain welds found materials together to create new forms. Sweet William *is made of parts of wrecked cars and is about 6' (15 m) high. The discarded material takes on new life at the hands of the sculptor. Los Angeles County Museum of Art.*

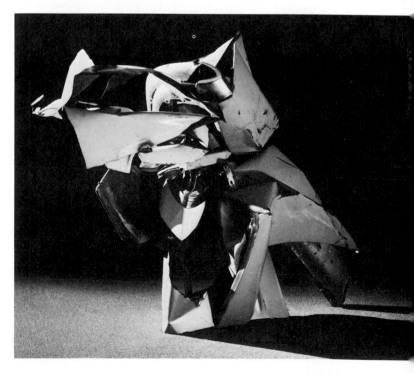

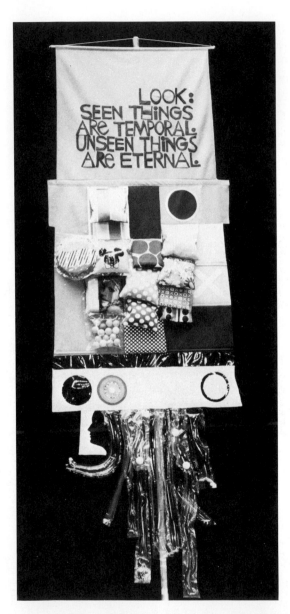

Richard Wiegmann's banner is a delightful combination of materials: stuffed pillows, plastic tubes, Ping-Pong balls, sheets of plastic and various fabrics. Today's artists and craftspeople are certainly not limited in the materials they can use.

Some Design Suggestions

Three-dimensional art is generally viewed from all sides. Some sculpture is created to go on a wall and be seen only from the front. These are *relief sculptures.* Work that is seen from all sides is often called sculpture *in the round.* When working, check often to see how your sculpture is progressing from all sides. Don't look only at the front. *Think* in three dimensions.

Traditional sculptors were concerned with volume and mass. They tried to arrange solid forms in interesting ways. Today sculptors are just as interested in the *voids,* the open spaces and the air around the work. Looking *through* a sculpture can be as interesting as looking *at* it. Sometimes artists use mirrors to put you into the work and make you a part of the sculpture.

Sculptures appeal to the sense of touch, as well as sight. They invite you to touch. When you are working on your own sculptures, take pleasure in how they feel.

Form and texture are important parts of your work. So also are color and line. When you are carving or constructing, be aware of the balance of your work. How can you check this from all sides? Think of the eye movement. Viewers will look at, through and around your sculpture. Think about unity, contrast and emphasis. The elements and principles of design can help you understand the direction your work takes. They can guide your work.

Try to make your subject and materials work together. Do not try to use clay when wood might be better. Do not use wood when wire is better.

The movement expressed in Kent Ullberg's Majestic Blue duplicates the leaping action of a swordfish. The 30" (77 cm) high work was first formed and carved in clay, then cast in bronze.

Robert Irwin installed his stainless steel cut-out on the campus of Wellesley College. It is shown here in winter and in autumn (detail). The work follows the contour of the hill, but remains flat on top. It is pierced with leaf shapes. When leaves are on the ground around it (detail) they seem to become part of the sculptor's creation.

Wood scraps can be carved, nailed, glued, sawed, painted, stained, sanded and varnished. You can build abstract or realistic works.

How to Get Started

Sometimes it is good to sketch a bit. This can give you the general feeling of your subject. For instance, if you are going to sculpt a beetle, look at beetles in books and magazines, sketching as you go. When you have settled on an idea, follow this procedure:

1. *Gather the materials and tools.* Be sure you have all that you need. If you have a kiln, then ceramics are suitable, but if no kiln is available, other materials should be considered.
2. *Decide on your working techniques.* If you have a box of wood scraps, decide whether carving or assembling would work best. Look at other sculptures to help you decide. Ask yourself such questions as these: Should I try carving a giraffe's thin legs, or would wire sculpture be easier to use? If I paint the finished sculpture, will I need to carve many details at the start?
3. *Begin Working.* Keep the major sculpture shapes simple. Add only enough detail to suggest textures or forms. Notice the balance. Notice interacting movements in the work.
4. *Use good crafts skills.* Do not hurry. Keep your work under control, so that you can enjoy the entire process of creating. Think about the textures, color and finish of the work as you progress.

Carving Sculpture

Carving is the oldest form of sculpture. New materials today have given it new life. Carving has traditionally been done in marble or wood. Today you might work in Styrofoam, plastic, plaster, soft stone or cement.

It is fascinating to carve. This is the only art form that relies on destroying and removing an original shape to reveal a new and finished form. In most carving techniques, you cannot replace what is cut off. Work very carefully. Be ready to make adjustments in your original plan.

Materials to carve may come in ready-to-work forms. You can try carving wet firebricks, blocks of wood or pieces of soft stone. Blocks can be prepared by pouring wet material (such as plaster) into forms and waiting for it to harden. Before beginning, be sure you have the tools you will need. These may include chisels, knives, hammers, sandpaper, files and mallets.

An Ecuadorian folk artist carved an old man and his dog from a single block of wood.

The polar bear was carved from a block of plaster which was poured into a small cardboard box and allowed to harden. You should keep plaster carvings small and use knives and files to work them.

171

Several of the mixtures listed on this page were used to make the blocks for these student carvings. Regardless of style, sculptors must show careful attention to balance, movement and contrast.

Several mixtures of cement, plaster, sand and vermiculite (or other insulating material, such as zonolite) are good to carve. Combined they become a material that looks like stone but is light in weight. You can carve it with a paring knife or another simple tool. Mix the dry materials together, add water until the liquid becomes very thick, and pour into a simple mold to harden. Milk cartons make excellent molds for these materials. You might experiment with one or more of the combinations listed, mixing them in a plastic bucket. ***Do not*** pour unused materials into the sink.

A. 2 parts cement, 4 parts vermiculite (or zonolite)
B. 1 part sand, 1 part cement, 3 parts vermiculite
C. 1 part sand, 1 part cement, 1 part plaster of paris, 4 parts vermiculite
D. 2 parts plaster, 1 part sand, 3 parts vermiculite

Plaster of paris can be used for carvings. It can be mixed by putting water (as much as the mold holds) into a plastic bucket. By hand, sift plaster into the water until a small peak remains above water. Mix carefully with your hands to avoid forming bubbles. As soon as it begins to set up (hardens), pour into a mold (milk carton). The mixed consistency should be like ***very thick*** soup. ***Never*** get plaster of paris in the sink, wet or dry. It can harden in pipes and block them.

Using soft stone, firebrick or one of the prepared mixtures, work with a paring knife to carve a non-objective form. Emphasize a smooth flowing movement around and through the sculpture. Rotate the sculpture as you work, so that it doesn't have only a front and back. Carve, file, sand and smooth into final form. You may shellac it and mount it on a wood base to protect it from bumps and crumbling. ***Use safety precautions when working with shellac.***

The animal is carved on both sides of the 1" (2.5 cm) pine plank and mounted on a metal rod. Edges have been filed and sanded for a three-dimensional feeling.

These forms were carved from soapstone by Eskimo sculptors. They stylized the animals of their environment into the simplest forms.

Other Suggestions

Draw an animal or human form on a 1"-thick pine board. Cut out the shape with a coping saw. Round the edges. Use woodcutting tools, a knife or chisels to carve low relief details into *both* surfaces. Mount it if necessary to make it stand alone.

Start with a prepared block of material, such as those mentioned above. Carve a simplified animal shape. Large animals with heavy legs (such as bears or elephants) work best. What other animals might be simplified into rounded forms? Animals that are lying down also work well in such sculpture.

If you have other carvable materials, such as fire-brick, softstone, lava stone or soapstone, create a simple animal or human form with few details. Select tools that will make your carving easy.

Ceramic Clay Sculpture

Forming animals and people out of clay was one of the earliest sculptural activities in history. You can easily see how a person might have picked up a handful of wet clay and begun to model it. Perhaps the form suggested an animal or person. The artist made some more marks, removed a bit more clay, smoothed out a few places and the animal took shape. A few final textures and features were added and the work was complete.

It is difficult to hold a lump of wet clay in your hands and *not* form something. The process is natural, because the consistency of the clay is easy to push, pull and model. When the material begins to harden (or dry out), it can be carved with wooden or metal tools. To make clay artwork permanent, the

dry clay must be fired in a kiln. Glazes can be added to provide color. Fired pieces can also be stained or painted.

Look through the ceramics sections of this book for help in understanding the ceramic process. Techniques and tools listed there can help you produce your ceramic sculptures.

Wet clay comes in several colors and textures. It ranges from low-fire clay to high-fire stoneware. Be sure you have a clay that can be correctly fired in your school's kiln, if there is one. *Grog* is prefired ground up clay. It can be added to your clay to make

Roland Sylwester uses various carved items to poke designs into his small figures. These three are designed to hold a balloon or flag (or some other item?). They are bisque fired, but will still receive a rubbed finish and another firing to emphasize textures.

it stronger for sculpting. Grog also adds an interesting texture and helps thick pieces dry better. Keep your ceramic sculptures covered with plastic to keep them moist. Dried clay is difficult to carve without breaking it.

If your sculptures are more than an inch thick in any place, they should be hollowed out. This will help them dry completely and prevent explosions in the kiln. Sculptures can be formed around one or more pinch pots (see the ceramic section). You can also use the coil or slab methods, or start with a lump of clay and start pulling and pushing.

Decorations can be stamped or scratched into the surface with special tools. But you may also use sticks, buttons, plastic or metal parts and other found objects. Glazing will add color. You may also rub the fired form with a stain to bring out the highlights. Look at the examples on these pages for ideas.

Start with two pinch pots about as big as your fist. Put them together to make a hollow ball. Invent an animal form. Add a head, legs and tail. Decorate by stamping, piercing or adding decorative pieces to it. When adding parts, be sure to scratch the surfaces that are to be joined. Add slip (runny, thinned clay) before joining, and smooth out the joints as you work. Simplify the features and forms. Don't attempt a realistic animal. Think about varieties of textures as you decorate. Bisque fire and then stain or glaze the work.

You may start with a single pinch pot about the size of a baseball. Use it as the basis of a clown's head. Add features and decorations. Mold them with your hands to exaggerate their proportions. Fire and color your work.

Start with a lump of clay and pull out sections for legs, head and tail. This can be the beginning of an invented animal or the simplified form of an actual one.

The fish and turtle were formed from pinch pots. They have been bisque fired and lightly stained. The ceramic shoes are delicately detailed and textured.

175

Other Suggestions

Make a ceramic purse, or shoe, or baseball glove, or another everyday item. Glaze or color the fired piece with acrylic paint or stains. Can you think of other familiar things that might make interesting ceramic pieces in this Pop Art technique?

Bisque ware (after the first firing) can be stained with thinned acrylic paint. Brush on color and rub it off with a cloth. Several transparent layers can produce interesting color surfaces.

Roll out a flat slab of wet clay. Use a wooden tool to cut the shape of a fish or a bird. Push various objects into the flat shape to create textures. Scratch the surface or add other flat slabs to the shape. This is a *relief sculpture,* so only the front side needs your attention. Decide how to finish the work after firing.

Ceramic relief sculptures can vary in style. The two animals below are carved and have designs stamped in them. The glazed sculpture above (from St. Andrew's Priory, Valyermo, California) has only slight depressions to contain the various glazes. Notice the stylization and simplification in each.

Not all sculpture is round. Joel Edwards has created a huge relief sculpture of flowers. It is made up of dozens of individually cut, decorated and glazed ceramic parts. Does this give you an idea for a group project?

The hamburger plate and the airplane have been glazed to add color. The bear has been rubbed with stain to emphasize the textural surface. Glazes often cover textures. They should not be used if texture is important to the work.

177

Constructing with Wood

The artist uses a chain saw to bite into a massive redwood log. The log is eight feet high and five feet in diameter. Noise, spraying sawdust and falling chunks of wood are part of the scene.

The artist holds a small piece of walnut wood in the palm of a hand. Fine-grained sandpaper gives a smooth finish to the form. It will be oiled and polished before the artist is done.

Both artists are sculptors. Both are using wood as their medium. But they are working in their own ways to express their own ideas and feelings in wood.

Wood is a warm and responsive material. It can be used in many ways. For centuries the only sculptural use was in carving, but that has changed. Contemporary artists *construct* wooden sculptures by adding piece to piece. Wood can be glued, nailed, tied, banded with metal strips, or stuck together with wooden dowels. It can be constructed to form sculpture in the round or relief assemblages that might hang on walls.

How might wood sculptures be finished? Why does wood have an interesting surface?

You can get wood in many forms, from toothpicks to huge logs. Scraps come in blocks, planks, logs and dowels. Can you think of ways that driftwood and other found wood parts can be used in sculpture? Some woods are hard: oak, birch, mahogany, maple. Others are soft: pine, redwood, fir, balsa. Some can be nailed. Others are too hard to nail. They require glue.

Gather scraps of wood that have interesting shapes. You might find spools, old door handles or

This totem pole is constructed of wood blocks, sawed and cut to fit a student's plan. Many tools are needed for this type of project.

scraps from your garage. Try the scrap bin at your local lumberyard for odd shapes. Check your school's shop classes for discarded wood that was turned on a lathe. Cabinetmaking shops might have interesting scrap pieces. Gather a box of scraps of different sizes and shapes to make your wood sculpture more interesting.

Assemble your scraps to produce a totem pole—a tall vertical pole with pieces added on the sides and top. Use glue or nails to assemble the wood. Remember that small pieces of wood will split if nails are driven into them. If you know how, drill holes in two pieces of wood and insert a wooden dowel to hold them together. Dowels can be glued to add strength.

This gigantic wood sculpture shows the rugged quality of wood. Huge beams were shaped with a chain saw, fit and bound by sculptor, Eric Gronborg.

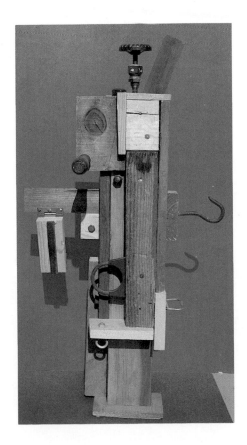

Raid the trash bin or gather scraps and materials to nail, screw or bolt into a happy mixed-media construction.

Start with your largest piece. Add pieces of wood in any and all directions. Or have the added scraps take a single direction. Try to create visual balance in your work, both symmetrical and asymmetrical. Which would give you the most interesting sculpture?

If your scraps are small, you might want to assemble decorative lids for boxes, or small sculptures.

Wood assemblages can be decorated with patterns, abstract shapes or imaginative designs. You can use tempera, vinyl or acrylic paint. If tempera is used, add a coat of spray shellac or varnish to seal and preserve the work. **Follow safety precautions carefully.**

Wood often has beautiful grain and needs no decoration. Varnish, shellac or lacquer can be brushed on or applied from a spray can. Some kinds of wood can be finished simply by rubbing with oil. You might experiment to find out what type of finish you would like to use. **Read and follow safety precautions with all shellacs and lacquers.**

Other Suggestions

If you use nails in your wood construction, can you make them become part of the design? Perhaps a combination of nailing and gluing would be best for your work.

Instead of constructing a totem pole, try creating a relief sculpture of wood scraps. Think of it as a wall decoration, with pieces projecting out into the room.

Decide whether you want your finished wood sculpture to be smooth. If your wood is rough, sandpaper it *before* you put the pieces together. It is difficult to smooth the whole surface later because of all the small corners and hidden spaces.

Turn your sculptures as you work on them. Keep them interesting from all viewpoints. A good three-dimensional form will have no front or back. It will be equally interesting from all angles.

Wood scraps, spools, dowels and found wood forms were combined to create imaginative lids for wood boxes. Students used collage and paint as decoration.

Interesting wood shapes can be arranged and glued to form a relief sculpture. These were sawed from various moldings, but you can also make your own shapes from wood scraps.

Constructing with Paper and Cardboard

It might seem impossible to *construct* with paper. We usually use it flat. We draw and paint on it, but seldom use it to sculpt with. Paper and cardboard are plentiful and come in wide varieties of colors, thicknesses and textures. They can be used to construct very strong sculptural forms.

Paper and cardboard can be cut into shapes. They can be scored (cut partway through) and bent. They can be rolled and folded. They can be glued (white glue or rubber cement) or stapled to produce structures with strength. Try to fold a single sheet of typing paper to produce a structure that will support this textbook. It can be done!

Use flat cardboard from corrugated boxes or medium-weight folio board. Cut it into repeated shapes, such as triangles, rectangles or circles. Assemble it into a sculptural form. You can glue the pieces on edges with rubber cement. Put the cement on each edge and let it dry. Then put the two surfaces together for a firm bond. You can also cut notches in the pieces and slip them together. You might add glue·for strength. You can paint and decorate the structure when it is completed, but it is not necessary.

You can produce large abstract cardboard forms using parts of large cardboard cartons. Cut them into irregular shapes and notch them deeply. Assemble your creation and add glue for strength. Cut holes in the large pieces, if you want, so you can see *through* the sculpture. Can you think of ways to use these forms in your school? Can they be used as a set decoration for a school play?

Artist Charles Gregson made this house out of scrap paper and cardboard. Several wooden parts were added to form the poles and banisters, but windows, frames, siding, stairs, shingles and trim are all of paper.

Cardboard constructions can be notched, glued or both on the edges. Corrugated cardboard or folio board can be used. The structures stand because of balance.

Students cut, folded, pleated, curled, scored and glued to make these paper constructions. Perhaps you have some ideas for paper work of your own.

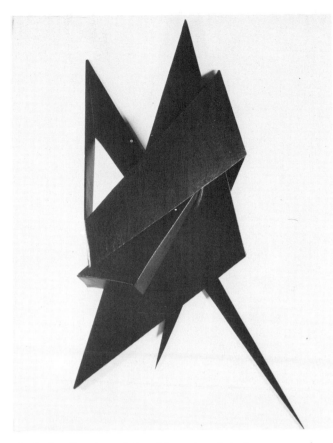

Other Suggestions

What kind of construction could you build if you had a large supply of clean cardboard cartons? How could it be decorated? Where might a large construction be placed in your school?

Design playground equipment for young children. Construct paper and cardboard models. Can the builders work from your model? What activities (such as climbing) interest young children? What materials might you use to construct models when the finished product might be steel, concrete, wood or plastic? Paint the finished model with colors that are attractive to little children. Create small cutout figures of children and place them on the model. This shows the size and proportion of the finished equipment.

Experiment with ways to bend, fold, pleat, cut and score paper. Use these methods to create paper sculptures of people, animals or abstract forms.

Carla Pagliaro's sculptural form is painted canvas and wood. It may give you some ideas. Can you add cloth to the work? How could color be added?

These imaginative playgrounds are constructed of paper and cardboard. Small paper figures add a sense of scale. How could children use these student-designed constructions?

Assemblages and other Sculptural Directions

Neon tubes, fabrics, metal sheets, glass and computers have become prt of the artist's world. Sculptors can use fur, hair, tape recordings, plastic and mirrors. If you use these or other materials to create three-dimensional forms, you are *constructing* sculptures. When various materials are combined, the form is called an *assemblage.*

To make assemblages you must be able to make the various parts stick together. Wood can be nailed, but steel cannot. Most artists use epoxy glue or other adhesives to join different kinds of materials. If you use special adhesives, follow the mixing directions carefully. *Follow all safety precautions.* Use clamps, tape or string to hold parts together while the glue sets. White PVA glue may also be used, but it is not as strong as some others.

What can go into assemblages? Anything and everything. You can make relief sculptures for a wall, or free-standing sculptures for a table or floor. You can use objects found in your garage or a junkpile. Interesting things might include buttons, sticks, watch parts, wood scraps, nails or bicycle parts. Old toys might find their way into your work. Perhaps you can use scraps from industries in your community. Are there good raw materials in your environment? Consider using stained glass, sawdust, bricks, wood scraps, plastic parts, fiberboard, wire or metal.

Assemble scraps to make toys, funny animals or abstract forms. Use acrylic, latex or tempera paint to add bright color.

Reinhold Marxhausen likes to make sculptural forms from unlikely materials. He used discarded leather harnesses at left.

Alexander Calder attached scraps of metal to a coffee can to make Chock, *a 28″ (71 cm) high imaginary bird. Whitney Museum of American Art, New York.*

Leo Sewell used hundreds of everyday items to construct Penguin, *a dazzling assemblage. It is 31 × 20 × 9″ (79 × 51 × 23 cm).*

Other Suggestions

Create sculpture in plaster of paris by spooning, pouring, dabbing, or somehow applying a very thick plaster mixture over a basic form made from wadded paper or paper and wire. The dried plaster can be carved, filed and painted if desired. Apply a coat of shellac to finish. ***Follow safety precautions.*** Wrap plaster-dipped strips of cloth around a wire form to produce a wiry figure. The addition of plaster and cloth makes a strong figure that can be decorated with paint and shellac.

Using a classmate or yourself as a model, cut features of the face (eyes, nose, lips) from cardboard.

Glue these to a heavy board cut in the shape of a head. Glue string to the surface to accentuate shapes or to produce line. Glue a sheet of aluminum foil over this and press firmly into all the cracks. Brush on thinned acrylic paint or India ink and partly rub away the extra color. This should produce a shine that will stress highlights of the low relief sculpture.

If you like to sew or use a sewing machine, you might like to make a *soft sculpture* by cutting pieces of cloth and sewing them together. You can stuff the form with bits of old cloth, kapok or shredded foam rubber. A paper pattern that fits together can make it easier to work with cloth.

Perhaps when you look through this list, you will think of other assemblages or sculptures. If you can get the right materials, try it.

Edie Danieli created Sandbag *by coating a regular brown paper bag with white glue and adding sand. She repeated the process until she produced a rigid sculptural form. Orlando Gallery, Sherman Oaks, California.*

These student sculptures were cut from Styrofoam. The one at left was finished with latex paint. The other was covered with Sculptmetal. Can you think of other materials to use with liquid metal or acrylic modeling medium?

Red Grooms builds gigantic papier-mâché environments. Philadelphia Cornucopia was created in 1982. Can you think of local historical events that could be developed into built environments, perhaps using other materials?

Kathlene Knipple's soft sculpture of a Berkel Scale is 24" (61 cm) high. It is made of batik cloth and stuffed to hold its shape. Orlando Gallery, Sherman Oaks, California.

10 Graphic Design: Logos and the Printed Page

Graphic design is a vital and ever-present part of our visual environment. Graphic designers are responsible for designing everything we read. They choose type-styles and layouts for television, magazines, books, brochures and advertisements. They work with words and pictures, type and visual images of all kinds.

This chapter explores three basic areas of graphic design: logos, type and page layout.

Logos

We confront logos everywhere! They are the basic symbols that graphic designers develop. Logos identify all sorts of companies—from multi-national corporations (Ford, Coke, Mitsubishi, Volkswagen) to neighborhood businesses.

You recognize the national TV network logos: the peacock, the eye or the *abc* letters. Some of these visual symbols (logotypes, or *logos* for short) become so familiar that we recognize them instantly.

Some logos are designed around letters or a single letter, such as the *GE* for General Electric and the GM for General Motors. Some companies rely completely on a stylized letter or lettering to identify their products. Think of the K for Kodak and the stacked VW for Volkswagen.

The distinctive lettering styles of Coca Cola, Oldsmobile, Cracker Jacks and many more immediately identify the products or companies.

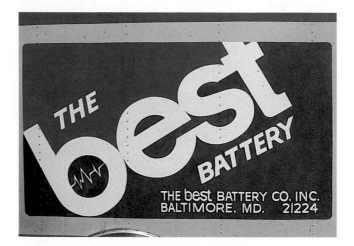

The logo for The Best Battery Company features the word best. *An electricity symbol is enclosed in the letter* b. *This is a well-designed and meaningful logo.*

Some logos involve symbolic emblems instead of letters, typestyles or words. Think of the star for Chrysler, the dog for Greyhound and the stylized globe of AT&T (American Telephone and Telegraph). Many airlines have symbol logos. Most of us are familiar with the walking fingers of the Yellow Pages logo.

Many logos are recognized in the United States and abroad. Small companies, organizations and transportation systems also have developed logos for use on their products, stationery and advertisements.

Easily-recognized logos are used by regional and national companies such as Warner Communications, Security Pacific Bank, National Broadcasting Company, the Rapid Transit District of Los Angeles, Volkswagen International and General Electric.

BULL & RAM INN
NEW CASTLE, RHODE ISLAND

the florist
1447 HOMWOOD, ATLANTA, GEORGIA

SAILMAKERS OF BOSTON
2784 NORTH MAIN CHANNEL, BOSTON, MASSACHUSETTS

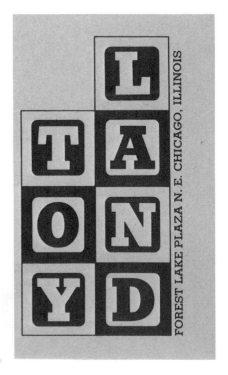

TONY LAND
FOREST LAKE PLAZA N. E. CHICAGO, ILLINOIS

Clip logos or identifying words or symbols from magazines and newspapers. Arrange an interesting display.

You may also enjoy redesigning existing logos that are outdated or unattractive. (Refer to chapter ten to see how graphic artist Saul Bass redesigned the logo for the Girl Scouts of America.) You may be interested in designing logos for existing companies that have no logo. You could make up an imaginary company and create a logo for it.

Begin by thinking about using your own initials in a uniquely designed logo. You can use color or black and white. Remember that it must be easily read and unique in design.

These logos were designed as advertising examples for the St. Regis Paper Company. They do not represent actual businesses. They may give you some ideas for logos you may design. Notice their simplicity and the immediate visual association with the companies' activities.

You may have strong interests, hobbies or skills that provide a symbolic log for you. Think of art, writing, music, sports, traveling, stamp collecting, sewing, hiking, reading or cooking. Can you design a logo featuring a stylized symbol to express this special interest?

Perhaps you can combine a visual symbol with your initials to produce a logo for yourself or your family.

Look in the Yellow Pages of the phonebook and study the logos. Choose several local companies that do not have logos. Design an identifying symbol for them. They may even be interested in using your design as their logo. The artwork can be large (perhaps 6" or 8" across; 15 or 20 cm) and done in black ink or color. Printers can reduce the size if your logo is later used on stationery or business cards.

Writer's Workshop
2581 Normandie Road
Los Angeles, California

Type books contain hundreds of typefaces that are available from typesetting services. The typefaces are cataloged by style and size to help graphic designers make the right selection.

Typography

Graphic designers usually work with two elements: words and illustrations. The obvious function of the words is to communicate information, and these words are set in type. There are hundreds of typestyles. Each style can be set in several sizes, weights and configurations. Type designers are responsible for the actual design, formation and characteristics of each typeface (style). These may be drawn carefully by hand or designed with a computer.

Every typeface has a name, such as *Pegasus, Futura, News Gothic* or *Corinthian.* The typeface used in this book is *Frutiger.*

Type is also a basic element of design. The typestyle and type size are important in the total design. The effectiveness of the copy depends on the typestyle, too.

Graphic designers have many typestyles from which to choose. They choose typefaces and sizes that are readable, appropriate and consistent with the rest of the design.

Some typefaces have serifs (small cross pieces at the ends of lines). Others do not, and are known as *sans serif* styles. A single typeface (*Frutiger,* for example) can be designed in variations that are **light**, extra light, **bold**, **extra bold**, condensed, extended or *italic* (see illustration). Type also comes in UPPER-CASE (capital) and lowercase letters.

If the work calls for extensive use of type (many paragraphs), the designer will have it prepared by a typesetter. For smaller jobs designers can buy type to rub onto the artwork or page layout. This kind of type is excellent for headlines.

Occasionally designers want unique styles of lettering and will have it done by hand. Or a job may call for fancy handlettering, known as *calligraphy,* that can only be done by an expert.

Words on a page are referred to as *copy.* The type size for copy depends on the space available. It also depends on the design of the page and the function of the words.

Headlines are usually set in the largest and bold-
est type.

Subheads are set in smaller type because they are
less important.

Body Copy is the main writing on a page. It is
usually arranged in text blocks, such as the ones
you are reading now.

Captions for pictures (also called *cutlines*) are
generally smaller than body copy. They might
also be set in a different type style or italicized.

The type used for all these purposes need not be the same style. All the styles used should look well together. You can choose by experimenting on sample layout pages. The graphic designer uses the chosen typestyle and size to create a type plan for the job.

The Helvetica typeface is available in fourteen variations. The right column contains the names and examples of several decorative typefaces that are effective on special jobs.

Helvetica EXTRA LIGHT
Helvetica LIGHT
Helvetica LIGHT CONDENSED
Helvetica LIGHT ITALIC
Helvetica MEDIUM
Helvetica MEDIUM CONDENSED
Helvetica MEDIUM EXTENDED
Helvetica MEDIUM ITALIC
Helvetica MEDIUM OUTLINE
Helvetica BOLD
Helvetica BOLD CONDENSED
Helvetica BOLD ITALIC
Helvetica EXTRA BOLD
Helvetica COMPACT

PEIGNOT LIGHT
PEIGNOT MEDIUM
PEIGNOT BOLD
Pendry Script
Playbill
Pretorian
PRISMA
PROFIL
QUENTIN
Revue
Ringlet
Rockwell LIGHT
Rockwell

Page layouts from magazines, brochures, catalogs and reports show a variety of approaches to this basic graphic design activity.

Layout and Page Design

When you open a magazine or book, you are looking at a double-page spread. Graphic designers usually work on these double-page spreads rather than on one page at a time.

The arrangement of text blocks, headings and visual images is called a *layout.* The planned arrangement of these visual elements is called *page design.* This is the basic work of many graphic design artists.

The purpose of page design is to create a visual unit that will attract attention and be pleasing to the eye. In the same way, architects design inviting buildings and fashion designers create appealing clothes. Page designers want their work to attract readers. At the same time, the page must get the messages across.

What you learn about page design you can apply to other kinds of layouts. Use your design skills on bulletin boards, posters, picture arrangements, library displays and scrapbook pages.

There are three basic components of page design:

1. the *shapes* that are to be placed on the page (pictures, drawings, type blocks).
2. the *space between* the shapes.
3. the *space around* the outside of the printed shapes.

Look at several double-page spreads in this book and identify these three parts.

The beginning designer should follow several rules to help provide the best page designs.

1. *Use a variety of positive shapes.* Photographs, artwork, copy blocks, captions and headlines, should be planned as various rectangular shapes.
2. *Maintain equal white space between the positive shapes.* This produces a visual rhythm. The viewer's eye will move smoothly across the page. The white spaces may be about ¼" wide, depending on the total design and the page size.
3. *Keep a variety of white space in the margin.* This will add interest to the layout.

There are a few more ideas that can help you design better pages. Refer to them as you begin your own page designs.

4. It is best to use rectangular shapes for pictures. Squares and horizontal or vertical rectangles provide enough variety of shape. Other shapes are often odd and distracting.
5. Do not trap large areas of white between positive shapes. White "islands" usually are distracting. They disturb visual movement.
6. Avoid vertical headlines. They are difficult to read.
7. It is easiest to put type on the outside of the layout.
8. There should be a *center of interest* in each page design. This may be a large photo, an art piece or a headline set in decorative or extra-large type.
9. Think of *balance* when you start to arrange the various elements. Balance the positive shapes, and balance the negative and positive shapes. This balance is felt or sensed. It cannot be mathematically computed.
10. Keep page designs simple and free from frills.

Layout Styles

After a great deal of experience, graphic designers develop layout styles that are unique and attractive. Beginning designers start with four or five basic layout styles. Read about them and try a few of the suggested projects.

All layout styles are composed of the same elements: positive shapes (pictures, text blocks, headings), interior white space and outside white space. A

Three graphic designers in a Sacramento design agency are working on layouts for a series of brochures.

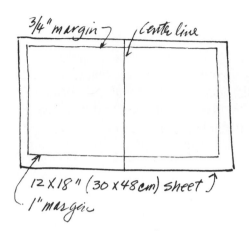

This is a sketch of a basic layout sheet (double-page spread) with margins and centerline.

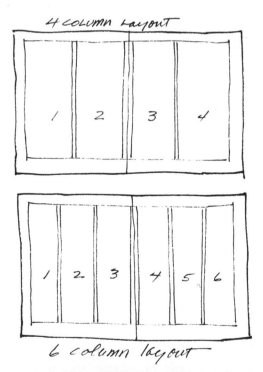

This is a sketch of four and six column layout formats. These might also be called two and three column layouts, if the designer is thinking in terms of single- instead of double-page spreads.

layout style is a system of guidelines that make layouts consistent and interesting.

Practice on 12″ × 18″ (30 × 45 cm) sheets of white paper. Draw an outside margin rule all around the sheet, ¾″ (1.9 cm) from three edges, and 1″ (2.5 cm) from the bottom edge. Draw a line down the middle. Use this format with several layout styles.

Column Styles

Columns are the basis for most page layout styles. Double-page spreads may be divided into four, six or more columns. These column styles are practical for several reasons:

1. They help establish a pattern that the eye can easily follow.
2. They help organize the actions of the designer and the reader.
3. They help the designer maintain a balance of photographs, text blocks and white space.

Whether you use four, six or eight columns, follow three basic guidelines:

1. Pictures should be fully 1, 2, 3, 4, etc. columns wide. Pictures should not take up only part of any column.
2. All text blocks should be one or two columns wide.
3. Headlines should take up full column widths when possible.
4. Establish a size for interior white space (such as ¼″; .7 cm) and use it consistently. Use it between pictures, between text blocks and between pictures and text blocks.
5. Keep extra white space outside the picture and text areas. Avoid trapping white space among the positive shapes.
6. Do not go beyond the outside margins unless you go all the way to the paper's edge.

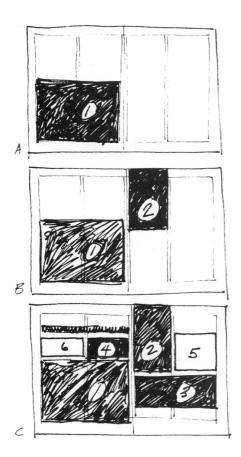

These sketches show development of a column layout style:

A.   Placement of the dominant visual element (two columns wide).

B.   Adding the second element (one column wide); The image shown here goes past the top margin to the top edge of the sheet. It is called a bleed.

C.   Adding pictures three (two columns wide) and four (one column wide). Elements five and six may be copy blocks or other pictures. The heading is sketched above six and four.

This is how a four-column layout might look. Try to figure out some other arrangements on scratch paper. The pictures can be different sizes, but must be one, two or three columns wide. There may be five or six pictures and less text. The black shapes indicate photographs.

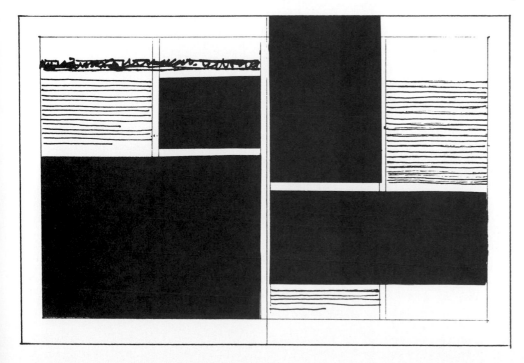

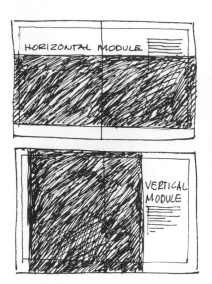

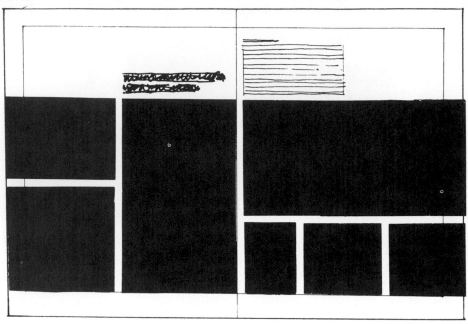

These are sketches of horizontal and vertical modular units. Other shapes and placements are possible.

This modular layout uses seven pictures that were carefully cropped and sized. The heading and copy block are placed outside the modular unit.

Copy blocks may also be included inside *the modular unit. This leaves a large white shape in which to place the title or heading.*

Modular Styles

Modular layouts are not based on columns. They are based on single large shapes. The pictures are grouped to form a single unit (module) that is either vertical or horizontal (see illustration). All text blocks are generally kept outside this large module.

A few tips for working with modular styles:

1. Pictures must be cropped to create even edges that form the module's boundaries.
2. Keep all interior white spaces the same size (try ¼"; .7 cm).
3. Choose a position for the dominant shape first. Then add the rest of the shapes, cropped to fit.
4. This is a good style when you have many small pictures.
5. Text blocks may be included *inside* the modular shape.

Mondrian Style

The Mondrian Style gets its name from a Dutch artist (Piet Mondrian) whose paintings were based on strong horizontal and vertical lines. Begin this layout design by drawing off-center vertical and horizontal guidelines (see illustration). This produces four unequal shapes.

These lines are guides for the placement of all the positive shapes (photos, copy, headings). Major shapes should be placed within ⅛" (.3 cm) of the guidelines, starting with the largest, most important picture.

Text blocks need not necessarily be the same width. They do not have to fit prescribed columns.

A few tips to keep in mind:

1. Outside edges of photos need not *always* go to the margin, although some should.
2. Keep interior white spaces the same size.
3. Mondrian layouts often make use of *bleed* photographs (pictures going past the margins to the edge of the sheet).
4. Headings and copy are usually placed *outside* the assembled arrangement of photos.

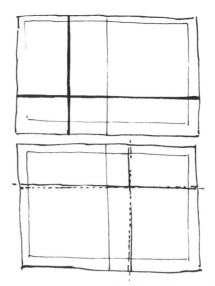

Mondrian layouts begin with two intersecting lines, each placed off center.

Notice the placement of the guidelines in this Mondrian layout. Equal white space is maintained inside the group of images, with varied white space outside the group. There are many variations in the Mondrian style.

In this sketch, positive shapes are put in order from one to six, to make sure they are placed properly along the guidelines.

This mosaic layout began with the large shape at the top. It was overlapped by the shape in the lower right. Can you list the steps that were followed to reach the finished page design?

This sketch shows the important sequence of positioning positive shapes in a mosaic layout. Follow the sequence in the text. Notice the angles (three and four) formed when number two overlaps number one. After the first four shapes are positioned, the rest (photos and copy blocks) fit into available angles.

Mosaic Style

Designing a mosaic layout can be compared with laying a tile floor. Start with the major shape near the central part of the sheet. Add others, keeping all the interior white spaces the same size. Try to follow a plan such as this (see numbers on illustration):

1. Position the major shape first.
2. Position the second shape to overlap the first.
3. Place the other shapes into the angles formed by 1 and 2.
4. Place other shapes (more photos or copy blocks) into the resulting angles.
5. Add the heading.

A few tips to keep in mind:

1. Outside white spaces should have different and interesting shapes.
2. Use a variety of positive shapes to keep the layout exciting and interesting.
3. Keep interior spaces the same size.
4. Tuck any necessary copy blocks and headings into the remaining white spaces.

Suggested Activities

1. Make small sketches of sample layouts. This helps you learn to organize visual materials quickly. (Thumbnail sketches can be 1″ × 2″; 2 × 5 cm).
2. Clip pictures, paragraphs and headings from magazines (they need not be related). Try different layouts on a 12″ × 18″ (30 × 46 cm) sheet of paper. Move them around in new arrangements. Crop the pictures and trim the text blocks as needed.
3. Design several pages (as in number 2). Use a glue stick to attach the pieces to an 18″ × 24″ (30 × 46 cm) sheet of white paper.
4. Make a bulletin board design, based on one of the layout styles. Develop it on a single theme.
5. Bring in photographs that you have taken. Arrange them in one of the layout styles. Attach them to a small sheet of black paper (10″ × 15″; 25 × 38 cm). Crop the pictures as needed.
6. If you are interested in page designs, work on your school yearbook. Yearbook page design provides excellent experience for future graphic designers and artists.

You can see part of the designer's rough sketch beneath the modular layout of this double-page spread.

11 Photography: Using a Camera to Help You See

Today technology helps us do many routine chores. Computers, telephones, television, radio, automobiles and jets help us transport things and communicate with each other quickly.

Artists also use technology to help them make art more quickly or accurately. New technical pens, airbrushes, reproduction equipment, calculators and computers are used in graphic design, industrial design and architecture.

Photography has become important in many phases of art. This is due to advances in photographic technology and availability of inexpensive cameras. Cameras can be used to create fine art photographs, to photograph other artwork and to record processes in creating artwork. Cameras can record detailed graphic information. Cameras and videotapes provide visual records of art and artists.

Cameras can be very effective tools. Gustave Courbet was an important French painter in the nineteenth century, when cameras were just being developed. He said with great joy, "The camera is my sketchbook." He photographed scenes, events, peo-

With special permission, two students are taking Polaroid photographs of objects in an art museum. Photographs provide visual information that can be studied long after you leave the scene.

ple, light and shade. He later used his photographs as he created his paintings. Cameras showed what the world really *looked* like at a specific time. The artist was free to create images based on that.

Today, artists and graphic designers use photography a lot. They use both color and black and white photographs. You can learn much about art if you have a camera and several rolls of black and white film. Use black and white because it shows light, value, contrast, texture and composition; and it is less expensive.

If photography is already your hobby, you may know something about the processes. Photography can be divided into three areas:

1. *picture taking* (with camera and film)
2. *developing* (processing the film to make negatives)
3. *printing* (making prints from the negatives)

For now, we are only interested in taking pictures. Equip yourself with a simple camera. Learn how to operate it. Get some black and white film and start looking for subjects to photograph. The next few pages provide direction and important ideas for your first photographs. You can:

1. Learn to see things around you more clearly.
2. Understand more about art.
3. Become more aware of your environment.
4. Learn to interpret your environment visually in your art.

A professional photographer (above) and an art student are using cameras for special projects. Teri Sandison is setting up her cameras and lights to photograph a food display for a magazine. She has an exciting career in product photography. The student is gathering visual impressions from a museum sculpture garden. The photographs will become part of a report on the sculptor, Auguste Rodin.

Form

Your black and white photographs can help you become aware of form. You can learn how to represent form in your painting and drawing. Students took all the photographs on these pages. They photographed an orange and some eggs indoors, where they could control the lighting.

Simple backgrounds emphasize objects. A single light source will produce dramatic effects. Several lights can produce soft effects. Notice how the shadows emphasize three-dimensional form.

How would you describe the edge between dark and light values? You can use this information in a drawing or painting. Look carefully at the shadow side of each egg and the orange. Can you see some reflected light? This is a detail that is often not noticed without a camera.

How has value helped show the three-dimensional form of the buildings? Would the edges and corners feel soft or sharp to your hand? How can you tell?

Set some objects in various kinds of light. Try window light, spot light and lamplight. Photograph them against simple backgrounds.

Values

In your black and white photographs, the values will appear in black, white and various grays. Look at the large leaves here. Notice how the leaves are separated from each other. How could you describe this separation in terms of value? Are the leaves flat or do they also show form? How can you tell? Are any leaves made up of only one value? How can you use this information in your own painting and drawing?

Study the tree branches in both pictures. How are they similar? How are they different? What makes this so? Which tree (in daytime or night) appears more three-dimensional? Why? In the daytime tree, do all the branches have the same value? Why not?

Look at the photographs on these two pages. What can you say about light, values and three-dimensional qualities on flat surfaces?

Take some photographs of your own. Record the qualities of light and value.

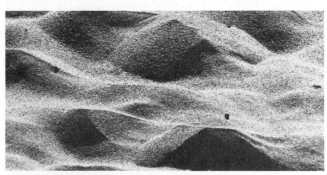

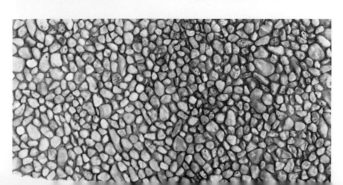

Texture

From painting, you know that artists can make or represent textures in their work. Of course, photographs of textures are only representations, too. Why? Study how a camera sees texture. You can often find exciting ways to make texture appear in your paintings.

Look at the natural textures shown here. Can you identify things by their textures? How are value contrasts necessary in showing textures? Why is the sand texture so different from the pebble texture? Notice that the leaves of each type of plant are textured differently. How can this be helpful as you paint and draw plants?

What can you tell about the textures on the old door? Is the surface smooth or rough? Painted or weathered? New or old? How can a camera help you make a painting of an old door?

Take pictures of natural textures in slanting sunlight (morning and late afternoon). Tree trunks, sidewalks, flowers, walls, fabrics and crumpled paper are good subjects.

Space

Photographs can help us learn how to represent space and depth on a flat picture plane. Look at the desert photograph. How does the camera record the different values of near and far objects? What difference do you notice in the detail? How can you use this information in a landscape painting?

Your drawing studies taught you about perspective. Remember the way parallel lines appear to lead to vanishing points. Take photographs that emphasize perspective. Show space in your photographs, paintings and drawings.

Set up a still life in the sun. Photograph it from slightly above it. This will emphasize overlapping forms, depth and shadows. Use a simple or contrasting background to emphasize the still life objects. This can help you learn how artists make paintings appear natural.

Reflections

Reflections in water and glass are usually temporary. They do not wait for you to finish sketches. The light changes or the water moves. Then the images are not the same.

Cameras can capture such brief moments and hold them for you to study. You can use photographs to learn how to show reflections in your own painting or drawing.

Look at the photographs shown here. Study the reflections of the masts and ropes. The actual reflection was moving constantly, but now it is still. How would you describe the lines? What can you learn about such reflections? Are they always the same? Do you enjoy the abstract, linear quality of the reflections?

A student took the photograph of two friends reflected in a puddle. The photographer was aware of her environment. Can you also see the shadows in the photograph? From where is the sunlight coming? Can you see the sun's reflection?

Notice a similarity in the composition of the two pictures. Can you comment on the importance of sunlight in determining the quality of reflections?

Detailed Information

When sketching objects, there may not be enough time to sketch details. The camera can help artists by recording details. Not all details **need** to be painted. But photographs are an important resource of visual information.

Study the details of the cannon and the steam locomotive. Look first at the large shapes, without noticing any details. Squint as you look. Try sketching these large shapes.

Now look carefully at all the details.

If you were drawing or painting these subjects, you would first squint and draw the big shapes. Then you would fill in as much detail as you wish. Probably you would not draw all of it. Note the texture, the form, the value contrasts and the focus.

Look at the sidewalk scene. Notice the huge amount of information captured in a small photograph. You can see signs, textures, shadows, perspective, clutter, reflections in glass and human proportions. Again, squint to see large patterns. Then study how the details interact.

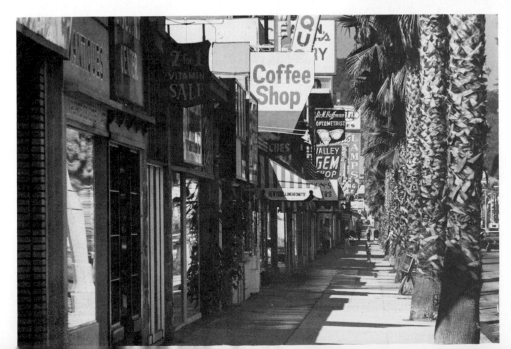

209

People

People, especially moving people, are hard to sketch. Since the camera was invented, artists have been fascinated by stopped action photographs of people and animals.

If you want to paint or draw athletes during a game, take a series of photographs. Study the angles, visual movement, balance and rhythms that only a camera can catch.

You can also learn how light causes faces and bodies to seem three-dimensional. Look at the contrasting light and shadow in these student photographs. See how the photographs emphasize the structure of the faces and the roundness of the forms.

Take group pictures. Try to catch your subjects in unplanned situations. The photograph of the coach is shot from an unusual angle. Looking at the picture, we feel that we are part of the action. Why is this so? What other visual angles could produce similar feelings? Try to take some photographs that will make your viewers feel involved.

Composition and Design

As you take photographs, concentrate on composition. Remember the principles of design: balance, unity, contrast, emphasis, pattern, movement and rhythm. How can you apply them to photography? How is this different from the way you use design principles in painting or drawing?

Photographers compose their pictures in the camera viewfinder. Move the camera around while you look at your subject. When you decide on the main point of interest, focus on that. Situate it in a good place in the viewfinder. (Try putting it off-center and not too near any of the edges).

It is easy to locate the center of interest in each of these student photographs. Why? Make a diagram to show the placement of the main point of interest in each photo.

Discuss the way the principles of design are used in these two photographs. Take several photographs that emphasize one or more of the principles of design. You will need to plan ahead for these photographs. It is hard to compose candid shots that emphasize principles of design.

Armco, Ohio, *Edward Weston, 1922. Photograph, 9½" × 7½" (24 × 19 cm). Los Angeles County Museum of Art.*

The Professional Look

Professional photographers have been getting excellent results for many years. Even so, there has been a tendency not to consider photography an art form. During the past twenty years, however, things have improved. Photographers have been exhibiting in major museums. Many galleries prefer to show only photographs. Commercial illustration now is using many photographic images. Darkroom specialists perform miraculous feats with ordinary negatives. And painters and sculptors are using cameras at ever-increasing rates as visual resources.

Many fine photographers are becoming as well-known as some fine painters and sculptors. Photographs now are sold at higher prices. Among America's well-known fine art photographers are Ansel Adams, Wynn Bullock, Dorothea Lange, Paul Strand, Peter Palmquist, Edward Weston and Cole Weston. There are many others, whose work is becoming popular.

Color photography can be seen in magazines such as *Arizona Highways, National Geographic, The Smithsonian, Architectural Digest* and other special publications. There are also marvelous books which emphasize color and black and white photography. Study as many of these as you can. This will help you become a better photographer. You will become more visually aware of your natural environment.

Photography is a natural activity for artists who interpret their environment. Use this activity to help you in your own art. Find your own way to save and file visual reference materials.

Coastal Textures, *Peter Palmquist, 1983. Photograph,
7½" × 7½" (19 × 19 cm).*

*This museum space is dedicated to the display of black
and white photographic images.*

12 Crafts: Making Art that is Functional

Crafts date back to the dawn of civilization. Even before recorded history, people created bowls, pots, urns, baskets and other containers for food and water storage.

Through the centuries, some people noticed that crafted objects could be beautiful as well as useful. We still enjoy elaborately decorated ancient porcelain produced by Chinese artisans. Museums collect the intricately painted urns of ancient Greece. And very old, finely-woven tapestries stand today as vivid visual records of past artists.

Today the term *crafts* covers many techniques and materials. Craftspeople now work in stained glass, glassblowing, metalsmithing, leather, ceramics, fiber arts, wood crafting and much more.

It is not possible to work with all these crafts in one art course. We concentrate here on jewelry design, copper enameling, ceramics, mosaic design and textiles. Work with this cross-section of crafts activities and develop your skills. You will form a base for later exploration of other crafts.

Remember, as you work through this chapter, that some craft materials can hurt you. Read label instructions on all the materials you use, and follow safety warnings carefully. Always work in a well-ventilated room. Wear gloves, safety glasses and approved respirators when necessary. Avoid breathing fumes or the dust created by your craft activities.

This huge rectangular bronze cauldron, 40" (102 cm) high, was produced by Chinese craftsmen about 3500 years ago. The decorations were meaningful to the people of the Shang Dynasty. The work was uncovered in 1974 in Henan Province, China.

Woven Belgian tapestries were used to soften the interiors of mammoth stone buildings. The tapestries also told moral stories, such as The Justice of Emperor Trajan, 1510. The piece is made of wool and silk and designed to hang in a courtroom. It is approximately 11' × 12' (335 × 366 cm). The Norton Simon Museum of Art of Pasadena.

Many crafts were made to enhance prayer. This Spanish processional cross (seventeenth century) is 42" (107 cm). It is beautifully crafted of silver and gold. Los Angeles County Museum of Art.

Greek amphoras were made for storage in homes. They also provided panels for painted decorations. This 18" (46 cm) vase is terra-cotta. It dates from 520 B.C. Dallas Museum of Fine Arts.

Sam Maloof carefully designs his handcrafted furniture from concept to finished product. Wood, grain, finish, fabric, color and detailing must work together to create such fine pieces.

Getting Started

Make a quick overview of this chapter and study the illustrations. Get to know the techniques, processes and materials in each craft. These questions will help you.

1. What is the purpose of each craft object you see here? Is it purely decorative? Does it hold something? How does the object fulfill its purposes?
2. Is the design pleasing to you? How does the surface pattern relate to the whole object? Does the surface pattern improve the beauty of the piece?
3. How did the materials influence the looks and structure of the object? Do the materials seem right for this use?

The student who made this batik design was concerned with technique as well as the design and arrangement of the dragons.

After your quick overview of this chapter, review the elements and principles of design. If *you* make a ceramic bowl, how might you use line, shape, space, color, value and texture? How might you use them in a mosaic table top or a woven wall hanging? Try to relate the elements and principles of design to the illustrations on these pages.

As you plan your design, choose a specific use for the objects you will make. Then decide upon its shape, surface design, materials and crafts process. Make several preliminary sketches to develop your idea.

Before you construct the object, experiment with your materials. Learn their characteristics. Practice the basic techniques that you will use. Then proceed.

The flat sides of Otto Natzler's ceramic piece are beautifully designed. The incised decorations and glazes work together to create a unified and splendid surface.

The porcelain pieces of Elena Canavier resemble sculpted underwater formations. They are designed more for appearance than usefulness.

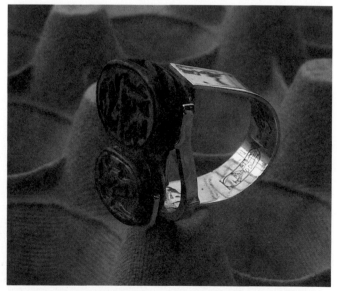

Joseph Gatto's ring is designed to hold two ancient stone scarabs. The design does not detract from the importance of the scarabs, but still holds them securely in place.

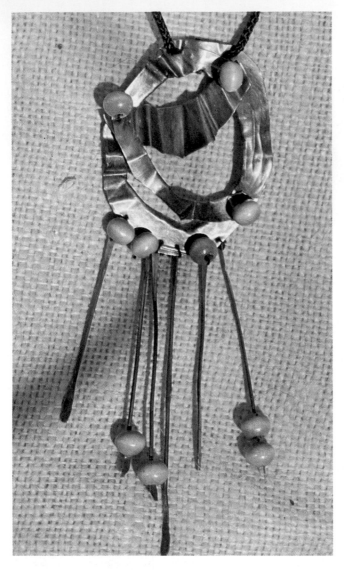

Jewelry

Metal Jewelry

The materials you will need are these: sheets and wire of copper, brass, and nickel silver, 20 to 26 gauge. Basic tools include heavy-duty scissors, a jeweler's saw, files, a bench pin, a hand drill, a charcoal block or clean fire brick, a propane torch, resin-core soft solder, abrasive paper, and 000 steel wool.

As you design a piece of jewelry, think about the qualities of metal. You can cut metal into shapes and join them with wire links. You can make the surface smooth or textured. A ball-peen hammer creates an interesting surface on metal. You can also make interesting textures by hammering metal on concrete or on metal screen. What textures and patterns can you create on a metal surface?

Draw your jewelry ideas on paper. If the shapes are to be cut from sheet metal, cut out the design and paste the paper onto the metal. Straight cuts can be made with heavy-duty kitchen scissors. To cut complicated shapes you will need a jeweler's saw. This tool uses tiny sawblades to cut metal; a size 2/0 or 3/0 is correct for metal of the thickness being used here. The blade is fastened into the sawframe with its teeth pointing toward the handle. It is important the blade is tightly strung. It should make a "ping" when plucked like a guitar string.

Use the sawframe with a wooden support called a bench pin. Clamp a board to a table top to improvise

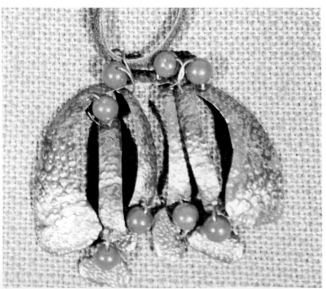

The two students who crafted these pendants used similar basic materials (copper foil, wire and wooded beads). From similar materials they created very different designs.

In this jewelry, the copper foil was tooled first and then combined with beads.

a bench pin. Set the metal on the board and cut with steady, even strokes. Do not put too much pressure on the blade or it will break. Do not twist the blade. If your shape has an opening, drill a hole, insert the blade through it, and fasten the blade into the saw-frame. To turn a corner, move the blade up and down in place, rotating gradually. Saw forward again when the blade is facing the right way.

You can see the drill holes in this metal jewelry piece. Starting from the holes, the student cut the linear parts of the design.

Brass sheets were cut to make various pieces. These were then linked with brass wire to create an attractive bracelet.

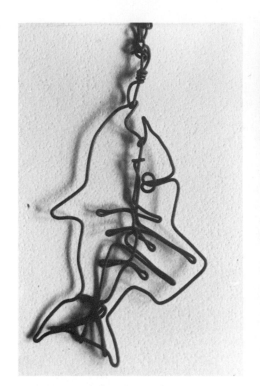

Wire jewelry can be made of many kinds of wire. The wire must be flexible enough to be formed by hand or with simple tools. The fish is a free-form piece made with easily-worked, black stovepipe wire. Notice the patterns formed by repeated linear designs in the silver wire jewelry. Tools are needed to create tight coils and repeated curves.

Wire Jewelry

Materials include 14, 16 and 18 gauge round wire in copper, brass, nickel silver and galvanized iron (stove pipe wire). You will need the following tools: wire cutters, round nose pliers, a ball-peen hammer and a steel surface for an anvil.

One interesting way to start working with wire is to create a coil to be used as a basic unit. Wrap a 6" (15 cm) length of wire around a thin dowel. This will create a spring shape. How can this type of coil be used in creating jewelry? Coil another piece of wire (similar to a watch spring or a spiral of rope) on a table. Use pliers to pull this flat coil out from the center to create a cone-shaped spiral.

Hammer a length of wire on the steel block to flatten it. How can you use this in your designs? Try making flat patterns with wire, then hammering them. The wire will hold its shape very well if you don't make it too thin.

What materials can you combine with wire to make jewelry? You can use fine wire to cage stones or chunks of stained glass. Create a cage by wrapping wire around your stone as if it were a package. Make a loop at the top to hang the piece as a pendant or earrings.

You can create jewelry from the colorful wire that is used by the telephone company. This usually comes in black, white, bright reds, yellows and blues. Visit your local telephone company to get some scraps (free!). Convert your found treasures into unique jewelry.

Plastic Jewelry

Plastic jewelry is made with a polyester casting material. This is a clear liquid plastic. A popular type is made of an epoxy resin (base) and a hardener (reactor). These two materials make a liquid plastic that you can pour into a prepared mold.

To prepare a mold, press or model a design in a block of plasticine (oil-based clay). For interesting effects try pressing nails, nuts or bolts into the clay. When the mold is ready, mix the plastic in a paper cup. ***Follow the label directions. Avoid breathing the fumes. Don't work near a flame or hot lamp.*** Stir the mix thoroughly and pour it over the mold.

What would you get if you dropped small pieces of stained glass, beads, pebbles or shells in the mold before you pour in the plastic? It's also possible to fill the mold part way, and then add interesting pieces. Pour in more plastic to fill up the mold. Invent other new ways to create plastic jewelry.

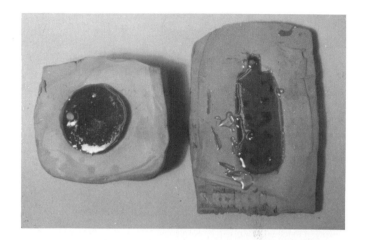

Simple clay (Plasticine) molds can be made using sticks, clay tools or found metal objects, then filled with plastic mix (top). Molded pendants and other jewelry can be combined with metals (or other materials), or can be used alone (bottom).

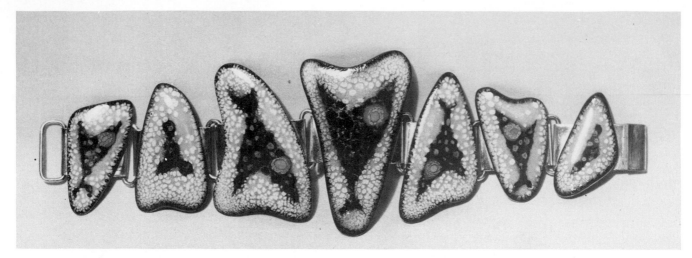

Virginia Dudley crafted this enameled bracelet of cut copper shapes. These were arranged and adhered to sterling silver findings. American Crafts Council.

Copper Enameling

Enameling is a popular way to make jewelry. It is also used a lot for making bowls, trays and many other three-dimensional forms.

First learn how to fuse powdered glass to a metal surface. Then you can design and make many interesting objects that are useful and decorative. Start by getting to know the materials and basic enameling techniques.

Materials include: powdered enamels in various colors, lumps, threads and flux (transparent, colorless enamel); sheet copper (18–22 gauge); copper shapes, such as squares, rectangles, circles, ovals, small trays or bowls; copper wire, round or square; emery cloth, steel wool, gum tragacanth and protective coating; needle files, jeweler's saw and blades and a bench pin and clamp; spatula, 80-mesh sieve, tweezers, wire cutters, round-nose pliers, hole punch, drill, bits and hammer; enameling kiln, firing fork, firing rack and trivet.

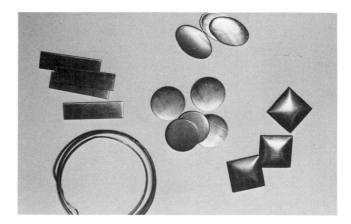

Copper shapes and wire.

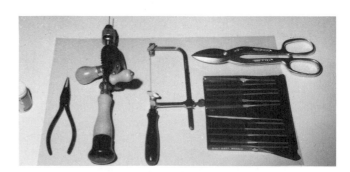

Pliers, drill, jeweler's saw, files.

222

The basic enameling process is visually outlined for you:

1. Use steel wool to clean the surface of a copper shape. Handle the metal by its edges to keep the oil from your fingers off the surface.

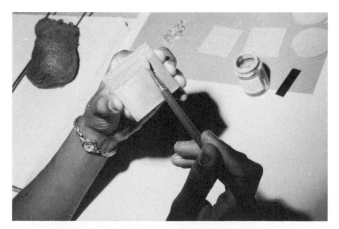

2. To prevent scaling or burning, cover the back of your piece with a protective coating. Use one teaspoon of salt to four ounces of water, or use a commercially prepared backing.

3. Coat the front side with a thin layer of gum tragacanth (Formula 7001).

4. Place the shape on a clean sheet of paper. Use an 80-mesh sieve to sift powdered enamel on the copper surface. Use a color you like. Get the powder layer as thick as a dime. Cover the edges thoroughly. ***Be careful not to breathe enamel dust. Wear an approved respirator while you work.***

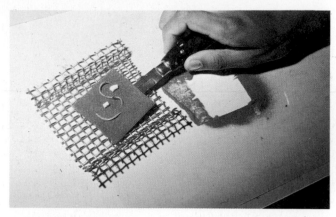

5. Coat the enameling kiln floor with a kiln wash. Follow the manufacturer's instructions. Preheat the kiln to 1500 degrees F (800°C).
6. Lift the shape carefully with a spatula and place it on the firing rack.

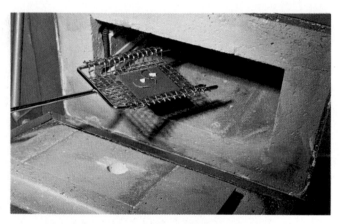

7. Using the firing fork, **carefully** put the rack and copper shape in a preheated (1500 degrees F) enameling kiln. Load the kiln quickly. Approach it from one side, rather than standing directly in front of it. This controls heat loss and prevents intense heat flow.
8. Fire your piece for about two minutes. Check the firing by opening the kiln door for a quick look. When the enamel is smooth and shiny, remove the rack with your piece. Allow your piece to cool and dry. As it cools, watch the brilliant colors appear, **but don't stand too close.**

9. When your enamel shape is cool, clean the back with an emery cloth. File the edges with a flat needle file. ***Do not breathe the dust you create. Wear an approved respirator.***

Variations on the Basic Process

1. Use a stencil to block out part of the copper surface. Hold a paper stencil over your copper while sifting the enamels. Use a second color on the blocked-out part. Try creating your own stencil designs.
2. Fire a solid color on a copper shape. When it cools, coat the surface with gum tragacanth. Place a paper stencil over this. Sift on a contrasting color. Remove the stencil and fire.
3. Fire a solid color on a copper shape. After it cools, coat the surface with gum tragacanth. Sift a layer of a contrasting color over this. Use a pointed tool, such as a toothpick or a wire, and draw a line design through to the base color. Fire. This technique is called "sgraffito."
4. Use copper wire to create a line design. Fit it onto a copper shape and flatten it flush with the sur-

Completion of firing.

These copper enameled pins show the use of wire cloisons.

A variety of copper enamel and wire jewelry.

face. Dust the assembly with flux and fire it. Mix a "paste" of enamel powders and water. Add only enough water to allow the enamel to be spread in place. Allow the paste to dry before putting the work into the kiln. Use the paste to fill the shapes formed by the wire. Fire. These smaller shapes, enclosed by wire, are referred to as *cloisons* and the technique is *cloisonné.*

These are a few basic techniques. Experiment with them. You can use them to make many copper enameled objects. Think up your own designs for bowls, trays, containers, bracelets, necklaces, pendants, pins, tie clasps, cuff links and buttons.

Decide what you would like to make. Design it and complete it. Use one of the enameling techniques described.

Review the metal-sawing techniques explained under the heading *Metal Jewelry,* in this chapter. If you plan to link shapes together, drill or punch the holes before enameling.

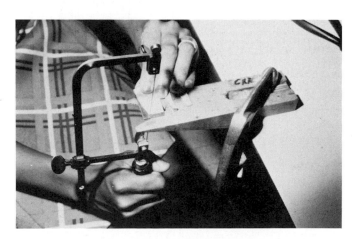

The correct form for sawing copper with a jeweler's saw.

Copper bowl and trays, vitreous enamels, by Vivian Sauber Koos. American Crafts Council.

Soldering

Some jewelry pieces, such as earrings, pins and cuff links, require special attachments on the back. These are called *findings.* Jewelry findings may be attached with epoxy or by soft soldering.

If you are going to solder the finding, clean the back of the jewelry piece. Use steel wool or fine emery cloth. Place your copper piece, enameled side down, on a charcoal block or fire brick. Clean the surface of the finding, too. Put the finding in place. Set a few small pieces of resin-core solder on the edge of the finding. Heat very gently with a propane torch until the solder begins to flow. ***Avoid breathing fumes. The art room should have active ventilation.*** After the metal has cooled, rub the back with steel wool to finish.

Ceramic Clay

One of the most satisfying craft materials to work with is ceramic clay (wet clay). This may be because clay is soft. It responds well to degrees of pressure. Clay is pleasing to work with because you can shape it and work it mostly with your hands. Your hands are the basic tools. In addition to these two rewarding qualities, clay can be used for a wide range of crafts projects: pots, bowls and containers of all kinds; jewelry and wearable ornaments; decorative tile for tables and wall hangings; toys, bells, wind chimes and unusual lamp bases.

Ceramic clay, prepared commercially, is often packaged ready for use. It is moist, soft and pliable. You should **wedge** the clay before you use it in a finished object. Wedging will get rid of air pockets, which can cause explosions during **firing.** Firing is the process of hardening the clay with heat. As well as preventing explosions, wedging improves the consistency and workability of the clay.

To wedge, remove a sizable portion of clay from the package. Form this into a ball by shaping and patting it with your hands. Using the wire attached to your wedging board, cut the ball of clay in half.

Put one half down on the wedging board. Now slam the other half down on top of it. Repeat this process until the clay has an even texture. Check the texture by cutting the wedged lump of clay in half and examining it. Wedge the clay until there are no more air pockets.

Now your ball of clay is wedged and ready. Try a few experimental activities to become more familiar with clay. Place a ball of clay on the table (clayboard) between two flat sticks that are ¼" (.6 cm) thick. Use a rolling pin or a large dowel to roll the clay out into a slab. The two sticks serve as a guide for the rolling pin. They assure you that all of the slab will be the same thickness.

The vases were made by two students who used different techniques (forming and finishing). Can you guess how each vase was made?

Basic Hand-Building Techniques

Traditional hand-building techniques include coil, slab and pinch pot (or pinch-pull). You can combine these. Another interesting technique is the press mold.

Pinch pot construction begins with a ball of clay. Shape it into a bowl form by pressing into it, pinching it and gently pulling the clay out. You can make pinch pots in many sizes.

Make *coils* by rolling small chunks of clay on a modeling board. Use the palm of your hand to create long, skinny pieces of clay. These are coils. You can make another type of coil by cutting narrow strips from a slab of clay. Construct a form by joining coils. You can layer them in rows. What other ways can you join coils?

Become skillful in *each* hand-building technique. Try combinations. Then incorporate your ideas into a handbuilt clay piece.

Look at the student ceramic pieces on these two pages. Can you tell which hand-building and decorating techniques were used on each?

Slab Construction

Slab construction is one of the most versatile hand-building techniques. You can make containers of many sizes from a slab of clay. Cut the parts, sides and bottom from a slab and join them.

Whenever two pieces of clay are to be joined, both must be roughened (scored) at the point where they will join. Moisten the rough areas with water or slip and press them together.

There are different kinds of molds that you can use to shape a clay slab. Choose a mold that suits your design. Roll a slab of clay and proceed.

Try using a plaster form (hump mold), a rock or an inverted bowl. Drape a slab of clay over one of these. Allow it to stiffen; remove and finish.

Roll out a slab of clay on a piece of cheesecloth or coarse burlap. Cut the desired shape, removing excess clay. Lift the cloth and slab together. Attach the cloth to the edges of an open wooden frame or box. The clay slab will take the form of the sagging cloth. Sometimes this is called a hammock mold, because the cloth looks like a hammock.

Find a cardboard tube, a mailing tube or a core from a paper towel roll. Sandwich a tube between two rectangular slabs of clay. Pinch the clay slabs on each side. How can you use this in a design? Try the same technique using two or three cores.

Try forming slabs of clay around wads of newspaper or around cardboard boxes and plastic bags filled with sand. You do not have to remove paper and cardboard supports. They will burn out when the clay piece is fired. When using a sand-filled plastic bag, position the bag's mouth so the sand can be poured after the form stiffens. Then gently pull out the plastic bag, too.

Press Mold

Plan a design and model it in clay on a flat board. Avoid having undercuts. They make it hard to remove the clay. Use heavy cardboard or wood strips to build a wall around the completed design. The wall should be at least ½" (1.2 cm) higher than the highest part of the design. Pour plaster over this to the top of the wall. When this dries, remove the clay. Allow the plaster mold to dry for one or two days. Now you can make several look-alike pieces by pressing soft clay into the mold, allowing the clay to stiffen and then removing it.

To achieve even greater variety in hand-building with clay, combine some of these techniques. Try combining clay coils and slab construction. Try combining slabs with a press-molded design.

Putting Personal Ideas into Clay

What can you design and then construct in clay? The answer depends on your imagination and your willingness to explore ideas. Don't be satisfied with the obvious. Aim for the unusual.

You can make containers. They might hold big things, little things, liquids or nonliquids. You might place them on a table or shelf. You might attach them to a wall or hang them from a beam. Your containers could have lids, spouts or handles. Containers can sit on a rounded base, on feet or on other projections.

You can make lamp bases, lights, bells or wind chimes.

Experiment with flat or low-relief shapes for wall decorations, slab masks, hot-dish tiles or a set of tiles for a small tabletop.

Use clay to make animals, figures and free-standing nonobjective forms. Construct a figure or an animal using the slab technique. You can make toys. Try all kinds of things, big and small.

Professional ceramists continue to explore hand-building techniques. Elena Canavier (top) rolls porcelain clay very thin, and then forms her dramatic bowls by hand. Notice the inside and outside finishing techniques. Otto Natzler joins several slabs to create simple and refined forms (bottom). He applies his own glazes that give the pieces glowing finishes.

A student constructed the vase by joining slabs of gray stoneware. She used clay tools and other implements to raise, lower and carve into the clay, developing the surface design. The vase was bisque fired. A walnut stain was worked over the surface.

John Goodheart used a press mold to make several self-portraits, which he then adhered to a wheel-thrown vase. The faces were stained. The rest of the vase was glazed.

The students who made these mosaic panels used enameled copper shapes as tiles. The tiles were adhered to a plywood base with white glue.

Mosaics

Mosaics are surface decorations. You can make them for a variety of useful and decorative items. Included among these are tabletops, room dividers, vases, lamp bases and wall decorations.

The required materials and tools are: Tesserae (tiles), ceramic, commercial or homemade; glass, Venetian or stained glass, pebbles and stones; wood, sawed, cross-grain pieces of dowels or wood scraps; and found objects and discarded items, such as jewelry.

For adhesives you'll need tile cement and white glue. You'll also need grout. Grout is a powder mixed with water to a creamy consistency. Grout fills the spaces between the tiles.

As supports or bases for mosaics, you can use Masonite, plywood or wood. You can also use three-dimensional forms, ceramic pieces or other objects.

The tools are end-cutting nippers, to cut ceramic tiles; a mallet or hammer and a canvas bag to break stained glass; a spatula, a putty knife and a tongue depressor to spread the tile cement.

Designing a Mosaic

Review the earlier suggestions for developing a design. Also review the elements and principles of design. Understand them well. This will be helpful as you consider ideas for a mosaic. After your review, sketch ideas and create your own design for a mosaic.

You may want to cover a tabletop with brightly-colored ceramic tiles. Or perhaps you would like to create a large wall decoration using a combination of wood tiles and stained glass. It may be better to start on a smaller scale, however.

Plan a design for a square or a rectangular shape with the largest dimension no more than 16" (40 cm). Think about your subject: human, animal, buildings, geometric shapes. Compare your first sketches with the mosaic materials you will use. Will you get the same kind of detail and shading as you get with pen and ink? How will working with ceramic, wood or pebble tiles differ from working with paints or wet clay?

In thinking through your design, consider the following points.

1. Do a broad, general treatment of your subject. Use little or no intricate detail. Reduce subject matter to flat shapes.
2. Mosaics have a flat pattern, with solid color shapes.

3. Aim for interesting shape and color relationships. Use contrasts.
4. Try placing the tiles close together. Now try setting tiles with larger spaces between them.
5. You can get different kinds of movement by positioning tiles in straight lines, curved lines or zigzag lines.
6. Think about the effects you get by cutting ceramic tiles into irregular shapes. Compare this with the mechanical regularity of manufactured square tiles.

Use colored construction paper to create a model of your design. You do not have to cut each individual tile. Cut just the larger shapes in your design.

Techniques for Making a Mosaic

After completing your design, organize your materials. Arrange your tiles by size and color in small boxes or cans. Cover the tabletop with newspapers. Have tile nippers, adhesive and spatula close at hand. Draw your design on the wood or Masonite base and proceed, using one of the two methods that follow.

Direct method Spread adhesive over a small portion of one section of your design. Cut individual ceramic tiles and press them into the desired position. As an alternative, you could cut individual tiles. Put adhesive on their backs and press into position.

Indirect method Draw your design on heavy paper. Make your drawing the same size as the actual mosaic. Cut the tiles and place them face up on the paper to match the colors and shapes of your design. Do not use adhesive.

Complete the entire mosaic, or a large section of it. Place moistened strips of water tape over the tiles, overlapping each strip. Do this very carefully, so that you do not move any of the loose tiles out of position. Put adhesive on your final mosaic. Move the

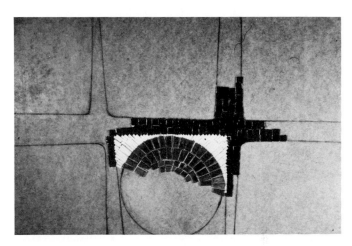

Direct method: Tiles are cut and adhered to Masonite on which a design has been drawn.

Direct method, using a single tile color: Colored grout, to be added, will emphasize lines formed by tile positions.

A.

B.

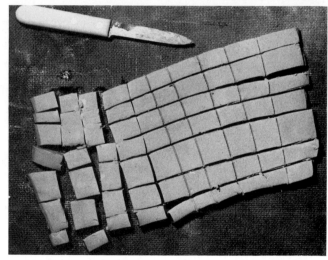

C.

Clay tiles can be made in several ways.
A. A design can be drawn on a rolled-out clay slab. The slab is cut into the required shapes.
B. Clay shapes can be textured and separated for drying, glazing and firing.
C. Tiles can be cut into different sizes that are stained or glazed and fired, before use.

tiles (held together by water tape) on to this surface. Press into the adhesive. After the adhesive has dried thoroughly, dampen the tape again with water and remove it.

Grout is a cement filler that you may want to use. If you place your tiles close together, however, grouting may not be necessary.

When spaces are left between tiles, plain white grout or grout with color added (dry pigment) can contribute another interesting design feature. Usually you should grout mosaics that will be used, such as tabletops, trays, trivets or bowls. Grout provides a uniform surface.

Mix powdered grout in water to the consistency of cream. Pour this over the surface of the completed mosaic design. Use a cardboard squeegee to work the grout into the spaces between the tiles. Remove excess grout with the squeegee. Allow the surface to dry. Then wipe the mosaic surface clean with a damp sponge or cloth.

236

This detail of a mosaic by Glen Michaels shows various materials that may be included in a wall mosaic. Notice the techniques for tile arrangement.

Textiles

There are many techniques for designing and making textiles. They all fall into two major categories.

1. Designs that are applied to the surface of an existing piece of fabric.
2. Designs that are an integral part of the fabric.

This section presents two textile design processes in each of these two categories: (1) fabric printing and batiking; and (2) weaving and macramé.

Printing a Design on a Plain Fabric

There are several printing processes for changing a piece of plain fabric into a designed fabric. Choose a process that suits your interests and your design. You

Students used traditional batik processes to produce these ambitious batik paintings. Many batik decorations rely purely on design, yet these two combine painting skills with batik processes.

can develop very exciting and colorful designs using fairly simple items. Try stamps carved out of wood, plaster or an ordinary potato. Wood scraps, spools, edges of cardboard tubes and other found objects are also good printing items.

Your success depends on design organization in the completed print. Even when printing with wood scraps or found objects, it is important to create unity and movement.

You might start with interesting shapes. Arrange them into a basic unit. Print the unit on the cloth at regular intervals. This will give the total pattern an organized rhythm. Try overlapping the shapes, changing colors, irregular repetition, or alternating two basic units.

In addition to the listed materials and your imagination, you need a piece of plain cloth; oil-based or textile inks; a brayer, ink slab, cleaners and plenty of newspapers to cover the work surfaces.

When the piece of cloth is printed with your original design, you might convert it into a table centerpiece. It could be a table mat or a wall hanging. Or you may wish to mat and frame it.

Printing with a Linoleum Block

To prepare for this project, study the textile designs all around you in draperies, clothing, furniture and wallpaper designs. What makes you like some designs more than others? Is it the use of color? The pattern of shapes and lines? Study the organization of the designs. Do you see a basic unit repeated? How is it repeated?

To plan your own design, make several sketches. Because you will be printing with a linoleum block, think how to repeat the print to create a pattern. You may wish to have two basic units, alternating two linoleum blocks as you print.

Materials that you will need include: linoleum block, cutting tools, block stop to hold the linoleum,

In this design repeated on cloth, note the half-turn of every other unit.

oil-based or textile inks, brayers and ink slab; cloth on which to print, such as cotton, linen or burlap; cleaning materials and newspapers to cover the table.

After you have planned your design, make a tracing. Reverse it and transfer the design onto a linoleum block. Cut the block, ink it and pull a proof on paper. Make several prints on paper first, trying different arrangements. Try overlapping, turning the block and using contrasting colors. Have you decided upon a pattern to use on cloth? If so, proceed to the final stage.

Stretch the cloth tightly on top of a thick layer of newspapers. Tape your cloth to the tabletop. Ink your linoleum block. Put it on the fabric in position for the first print and press hard. Remove the block by lifting it *straight* up. Continue printing until your design is complete. Should you ink the block before every printing?

Relief blocks may also be made from wood, Styrofoam or a surface built up with cardboard shapes.

Preliminary sketches and drawings are ready to be transferred to a linoleum block.

The linoleum block is cut and ready for printing.

Printing with a Silk-Screen

You will need a frame with silk stretched tightly; squeegee, silk-screen inks (oil-based); cloth to print (cotton, muslin, burlap); stencil film, adhering fluid; cleaners, stencil knife and old newspapers.

Silk-screen printing is a stencil process. The screen is silk stretched on a wood frame. The screen is converted into a stencil. Inks are forced through the screen to make a print on a surface below. The screen is prepared by blocking portions of the silk. The ink won't go through these areas. Areas to be printed are left open so that ink can pass through. Review the printmaking section of Chapter Eight.

There are several methods for converting a clean silk-screen into a printing stencil. These pages illustrate one method: the use of stencil film. Stencil film is a commercial film of colored lacquer. It is laminated to a sheet of glassine.

Plan your design, following the same steps as for linoleum-block printing. Think about the use of shape and contrasting colors in your design. Place your design on a flat surface under a sheet of stencil film. Follow the lines of your design with a stencil knife and cut through the lacquer part of the film. Do not press too hard on the knife or you will cut the backing sheet of glassine. Peel off the areas to be printed. Then place the cut stencil on a pad of newspapers. Put the clean silk-screen over it. Apply adhering fluid to the screen with a cloth. **Be sure the artroom is well ventilated when you use adhering fluid.** Rub briskly with a dry cloth. After the film has dried to the silk-screen, remove the glassine backing. Fill in the open areas around the film with paper tape. The screen stencil is ready for printing.

Stretch your cloth tightly over a padding of newspapers. Place the screen over the cloth where you want to make the first print. Have a classmate hold the screen firmly in place. Pour some silk-screen ink onto one end of the screen. Using a squeegee, pull the ink across the stencil to the other end. Remove the screen and position it on the cloth for the next print. Continue this procedure until you have completed your design.

The design repeats to create pattern and a new design.

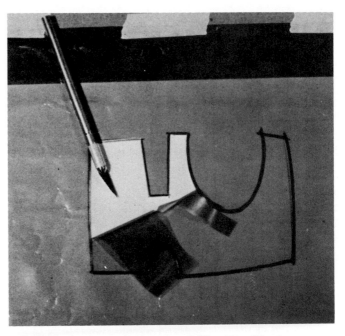

The design is beneath the stencil film. The film is partially cut.

Here the film stencil is adhered to the silk-screen, ready to print.

The design is silk-screened on cloth to form a repeating pattern.

Designing With Batik

Traditionally, batik is designing on cloth using wax and dyes. The design is drawn with a tjanting or painted on the cloth with wax. The cloth is then immersed in dye. The unwaxed areas receive the color. More wax is applied and the cloth is put into a dye of a different color. The second color should be darker than the first. This procedure is repeated until the design is completed. Remove the wax by boiling the cloth in water or placing the design between sheets of newsprint and pressing with a warm iron (repeat until all the wax is removed).

The crackled effect characteristic of batik is made by balling the cloth tightly after each waxing, before the dye bath.

A simple approach to batik design needs only one dye bath and uses colored wax crayons instead of clear wax. The materials needed are colored wax crayons; a dark household dye; a muffin tin with eight or more sections; an electric hot plate; a large pan; a large can or bucket for the dye; an electric iron; several bristle brushes (one for each color to be used) and a washed cotton cloth on which to design.

Plan your design. Place small chunks of wax crayons in sections of the muffin tin, one color in each section. Place the muffin tin in a pan of water on the hot plate. As the water heats up, the crayons will melt. Tape your plain cloth to the table, over a padding of newspapers. Paint your design with the melted wax crayons. Use the bristle brushes, one for each color. Plan to leave parts of the cloth unpainted. When your wax crayon design is finished, ball the cloth, crackling the wax crayon colors. Open the cloth and immerse it in the dark dye bath. After the dye has taken, remove the cloth and hang it to dry. When dry, place the cloth flat between newsprint and press with a warm iron. Repeat this step several times to remove most of the wax. The result should be brilliant colors with the crackled effect of a batik.

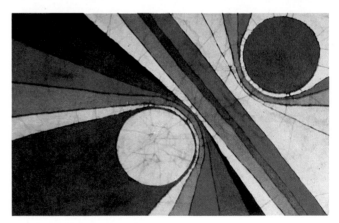

These student batik designs reflect traditional and contemporary techniques and subjects.

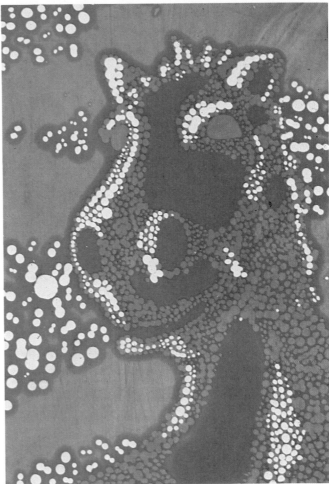

Weaving and Macramé

Weaving on a Box Loom

The basic principle of weaving is the interlacing of threads called **weft,** with other threads, called **warp.** Essentially, weaving is the running of weft threads over and under a number of warp threads to create a design.

The first step in the weaving process is to arrange the warp threads on a loom.

There are many different types and sizes of looms. You can attach warp threads to a single dowel or to cardboard shapes, frames or boxes. Or you could use more complicated table and floor looms.

The *box loom* is easy to construct and is best for practicing basic weaving techniques. Materials include a large wooden box with an open top, warp thread (heavy cord), various colors of yarn and 1" (2.5 cm) flat-head nails.

Hammer a row of flat-head nails across two opposite ends of the box. They should be spaced ¼" to ½" (.6 cm to 1.2 cm) apart and hammered halfway into the wood. Tie the warp thread to the first nail at one end. Stretch it across and around the first two nails at the opposite end; then, back and around the second and third nail of the starting end. Continue back and forth until all the nails are used and the warping is complete. You should end up with a number of warp threads arranged tightly and parallel to each other across your box loom.

You are now ready to weave. Start with a single color of yarn. According to your design, move it over one warp thread and under another across the width of the loom. Then return it the other way. After several movements across the loom, your woven design will become a shape. Try another color of yarn. What are some ways that you can change this basic technique to create other effects?

As you become more skilled, experiment with other materials for the weft, such as ribbon, raffia, twigs or feathers. Leave open spaces, tie knots or insert beads and buttons.

The box loom is a very useful piece of equipment for weaving placemats, wall hangings and other decorative items. However, you may wish to try your weaving skills on other kinds of looms.

The weaving on this box loom is partly finished.

Macramé

Designing with knots is known as macramé. It usually produces interesting patterns using cords of different sizes and colors, such as yarn, jute and rope. Jewelry, bags, clothing and decorative items, such as wall hangings, may be made with macramé.

There are no rigid rules for macramé design. Your imagination and a few basic knots can produce many exciting designs.

The basic structure of macramé is knotted cords. Their arrangement is your creative work.

Knotting cords may be mounted on a holding cord, a dowel or even a tree branch. These cords should be three or four times as long as the design that you are knotting. The number of knotting cords will determine the width of your design.

An orange crate is converted into a two-sided loom. The warp is wrapped around the box, guided by notches in the wood. The advantage of this type of box is that the one-piece woven cloth can be easily made into a pillow or handbag.

A gallery of student weavings shows some of the possible variations. The basic weaving techniques have already been learned.

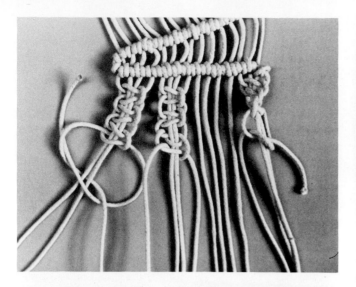

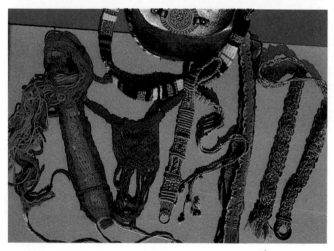

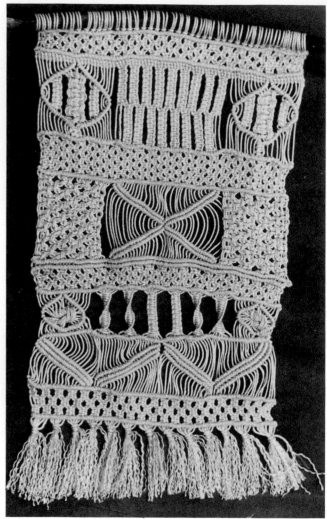

A macramé belt (top) is shown unfinished. You can see how the knots are being formed as the work progresses. A selection of student work, both macramé and weaving, can be seen in this colorful display (bottom). Does this give you ideas for work of your own?

Materials include a work board, nails (or pins) and cord. Sieve cord no. 6 and pearl cotton no. 3 are usually used for jewelry; macramé cord, jute tone and roving for belts and wall hangings. But you can use almost any cord, even rope, depending upon the desired effect.

Try a practice piece. Fasten the holding cord across one end of your work board. Mount several (12, 16 or 20) knotting cords on the holding cord by looping them around and pulling the two loose ends tightly through the loop. You have just made a number of double reverse half hitches. Drive a nail, at each half hitch, part of the way into your work board. Lay the first cord right or left across the other cords. Tie double half hitches over it with each of the remaining cords. Keep the knot-bearing cord taut while you do this. Why don't you try doing this halfway across

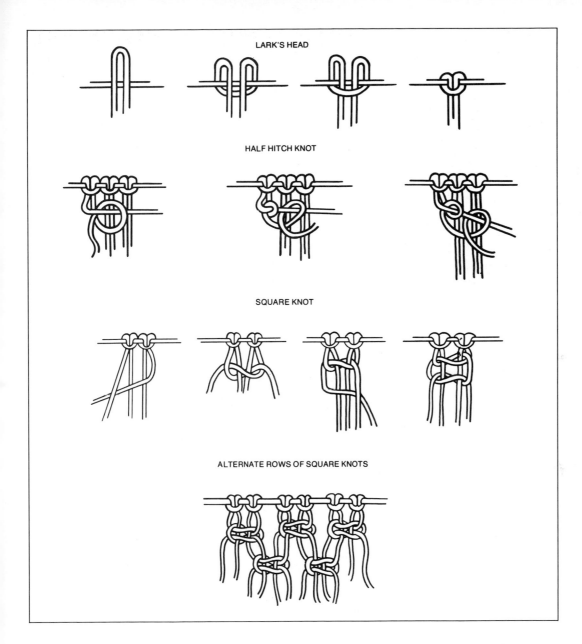

LARK'S HEAD

HALF HITCH KNOT

SQUARE KNOT

ALTERNATE ROWS OF SQUARE KNOTS

from the left and then do the same thing using the last cord on the right?

Knot a couple of rows across, using the double half hitch. Divide the cords into sections, four cords to each and tie a series of square knots vertically. Now go back to the double half hitch and knot a couple more rows horizontally. Returning to the sections, knot a series of half knots.

Keep it up. Think of ways you can interlace the cords and knot them. Leave open spaces. Collect a group of cords and tie them. Try some new knots, invent your own variations.

By now you may be thinking of a specific item you would like to macramé. Determine its size and use and proceed. For added interest, plan to put beads, rings, buttons, shells or stones into your macramé.

Glossary

abstract art   a style of art that uses simplified arrangements of shape, line, texture and color, often geometric to depict people, places or objects. *Abstract* may refer to nonobjective art.

Abstract Expressionism   a twentieth-century painting style that expresses feelings and emotions through slashing, active brushstrokes. Often called *Action Painting*.

acropolis   the highest point of any ancient Greek city and the site of the temples. The *Parthenon* is on the acropolis in Athens.

aesthetic   dealing with the nature of beauty and artistic judgments.

aqueduct   a long, continuous trough built by the ancient Romans to bring water from the mountains to cities by gravity. The aqueducts crossed valleys on tall bridges that included arches.

architect   a person who designs and creates plans for buildings, groups of buildings or communities.

architecture   the design of buildings, such as homes, offices, schools, industrial structures.

artifacts   objects usually simple, that were created or adapted by people.

assemblage   artwork that includes various three-dimensional objects. It can stand on the floor or hang on a wall.

asymmetrical balance   a type of visual balance in which the two sides of the composition are different yet balanced; visually equal without being identical.

Avant Garde Art   the style of *contemporary* art at any time. It is the newest form of visual expression, and farthest from traditional ways of working.

balance   a principle of design that refers to the equalization of elements. There are three kinds of balance: symmetrical (formal), asymmetrical (informal) and radial.

Baroque   a period of time (1600s) and style of art that stressed swirling action, large works of art and elaborate detail and richness, even in drawing.

basilica   an ancient Roman building (long and narrow) that served as a meeting place and judgement hall. Later, the Christians used the basilica style for their churches.

Bauhaus   A German art school, begun in 1918, that stressed science and technology as major resources for art and architecture.

bisque ware   a clay object that has been fired to appropriate temperature in a kiln.

brayer   a small roller used to spread printing ink on a linoleum block or wood block before printing.

Byzantine Art   the art style of Byzantium, using a lot of gold and mosaic in church decorations.

Byzantium   an ancient Greek and Roman city on the Bosporus, now called Istanbul, Turkey. Constantine used it as the capital of the Eastern Roman Empire from 330 A.D., and changed its name to Constantinople.

cathedral   a large church for the congregation of a Roman Catholic Bishop. It contains his throne, called a *cathedra*.

ceramic jewelry   jewelry made from wet clay.

chroma   an element of design that relates to the brightness and dullness of a color.

cityscape   a painting or drawing that uses elements of the city (buildings, streets, shops) as subject matter.

collage   a technique in which the artist glues material (paper, cloth, found objects) to a background.

color   an element of design that identifies hues.

combine painting a type of painting begun in the twentieth century. The artist combines real objects (shirt, book, stuffed animal) with painted areas.

communication letting others know what you are thinking, saying and feeling. Communication may be verbal, visual, musical or physical.

composition the arrangement of the parts in a work of art, usually according to the principles of design.

conceptualized art a style of painting or sculpture. The artist communicates a general idea, not how the subject actually looks. An African tribal mask is a conceptualized face.

construction a product in which parts are added together to complete the work.

constructivism a style of art (1913) that stressed the three-dimensional, abstract arrangement of metals, glass, plastics and/or wire.

contemporary of the present time or style.

contrast a principle of design that refers to differences in values, colors, textures and other elements in an artwork. Contrast is used to achieve emphasis and interest.

contour drawing a single-line drawing that defines the outer and inner forms (contours) of the subject.

crafts a form of art expression through creation of useful objects. Can include fiber arts, ceramics and metal smithing.

craftsperson an artist who designs and creates useful objects such as textiles, ceramics and jewelry.

crayon etching a technique in which crayon is applied heavily to a ground, then covered with an opaque ink or paint. Designs are scratched (etched) through the covering material to the colored crayon below.

Cubism a style of art in which the subject is broken and reassembled in an abstract form, emphasizing geometric shapes.

culture those elements that add to the aesthetic aspects of our lives, enriching them with beauty and enjoyment.

dynasty a period of time in which a single family has dominance over a people, such as the Ming Dynasty in China.

emphasis a principle of design by which the artist or designer may use opposing sizes or shapes, contrasting colors or other means to draw greater attention to certain areas in a work of art.

etching a printmaking technique that transfers the inked image to paper from lines cut in a metal (or plastic) plate. The process needs a strong press.

expressionism any style of art in which the artist tries to communicate strong personal and emotional feelings. If written with a capital "E," it refers to a definite style of art begun in Germany early in the twentieth century.

fashion illustrator a person who draws fashion designs for advertisements in magazines and newspapers.

Fauvism a style of painting, started in France, in which the artist communicates feelings through a personal use of color, usually bright and intense.

firing the heating of ceramic clay in a kiln to harden the clay object.

fixative a substance that is sprayed over charcoal, pastel or pencil drawings to make those materials adhere permanently to the paper and to prevent smearing.

flying buttress a feature of Gothic architecture made up of a tower buttress, standing away from the wall of the church, and a flying arch, connecting the buttress to the wall.

form an element of three-dimensional design (cube, sphere, pyramid, cylinder and free flowing) enclosing volume. Contrasts with the design element *shape*, which is two-dimensional (flat).

fresco a painting technique in which artists apply wet colored plaster to a wet plaster wall. A type of mural painting.

forum the center of a Roman city used as marketplace, for assemblies and for other business.

geometric art art that uses lines and shapes that recall geometry: triangles, squares, rectangles, straight lines, arcs, circles.

Gothic Art the art of Europe (1150 to 1400) mainly associated with church construction. It centered in France and spread over the continent. It is characterized by pointed arches, flying buttresses, stained glass windows and overall unity of construction.

Gothic arch a pointed arch, developed to allow greater height in building and huge window spaces in Gothic churches.

gouges scoop-shaped tools used for removing linoleum or wood when making relief print blocks of these materials.

graphic artist a person who designs packages and advertisements for newspapers and magazines; illustrates for ads, books, magazines; draws cartoons; designs displays and signs; produces any kind of art for reproduction.

greenware a clay piece that has dried, usually at room temperature.

grog fired stoneware that is ground and added to fresh wet clay to give it more body and texture.

ground the surface on which two-dimensional artwork is done, such as paper, canvas, cardboard.

hard edge painting   a style of art in which the artist uses crisp, clean edges and applies the values or colors so that they are even and flat.

horizontal line   an actual or imaginary line that runs across the work defining the place where sky and earth come together.

horizontal   a line or shape that is parallel to the top and bottom edges of the paper.

hue   the name of a color, such as yellow, yellow-orange, blue-violet, green.

icon   a sacred painting or image. Usually it portrays Jesus or one or more saints. Frequently done in enamel or egg tempera paint.

impressionism   a style of drawing and painting (1875 and following) begun in France, that stresses a candid glimpse of the subject, and emphasizes the momentary effects of light on color.

incised lines   very thin lines cut into the surface of a printing plate, such as in etchings or woodcuts.

jewelry   ornamental objects to be worn: rings, earrings, pendants, necklaces, bracelets.

kiln (ceramic)   an oven-like piece of equipment used to fire clay objects at high temperatures.

kneading   a technique used to prepare clay. Air is removed from the clay to obtain uniform consistency.

landscape   a work of art that shows the features of the natural environment (trees, lakes, mountains, flowers).

line   an element of design that may be two-dimensional (pencil or paper), three-dimensional (wire or rope) or implied (the edge of a shape or form).

linoleum cut   a relief print made from a piece of linoleum. The areas and lines that are cut out will remain unprinted. The original surface will transfer ink to the paper.

loom   equipment used in weaving. There are many types, from a simple cardboard loom to a four-heddle floor loom.

medium   a material used to create artwork. Plural is media.

metropolitan region   a large settled area of dwellings and industries that includes a city and its surrounding towns, villages and suburban developments.

mirror image   the "flopped-over" picture that occurs when prints are made from linoleum, wood or metal plates. Words are printed in reverse, for example.

mixed media   a two-dimensional technique that uses more than one medium; for example, a crayon and watercolor drawing.

mobile   a movable and balanced sculpture, suspended from above, that turns and rotates as it is hit by moving air.

modeling   working with clay or other materials to form three-dimensional sculptures.

monoprint   a print in which there is only one copy created. Many techniques can be used to transfer the original design to paper, but the same design cannot be repeated.

mosaics   designs or pictures made with squarish cut shapes of glass or colored stone. Mosaics can also be made of paper, natural materials, wood or cardboard.

movement   a principle of design that refers to the arrangement of parts in a drawing to create a slow-to-fast flow of your eye through the work.

mural   a large painting, made to be permanent on a wall.

mythology   the stories told in ancient Greek and Roman cultures about their gods and goddesses. These figures still are subjects for paintings and sculptures.

nature print   a print made by rolling ink on natural objects (leaves, flowers, grass) and pressing out on paper.

negative space   the area around the objects in a painting, and the space around the solid parts of a sculpture.

Neo-Classic   a style of art (begun about 1850) in which artists worked in the styles of ancient Greece and Rome; a revival of classic styles.

Nonobjective art   art with no recognizable subject matter. The real subject is the composition of the drawing or painting itself.

Op Art (Optical Art)   a style of art (mid–twentieth century) that uses optical (visual) illusions of many types. These works of art are composed to confuse, heighten or expand visual sensations.

opaque   material that will not let light pass through; the opposite of transparent.

organic   free form, or a quality that resembles living things; the opposite of mechanical or geometric.

painterly quality   that aspect of artwork that allows brush-strokes to show and let us see what the artist's movements were.

paper pulp   modeling material made by mixing small bits of paper in water and wheat paste.

papier-mâché   a technique for working with paper (strips or pulp) and glue or paste, to form three-dimensional sculptures or reliefs. It produces a solid material that is quite strong when dry.

pattern   a principle of design. Combinations of lines, colors and shapes are used to show real or imaginary things. Also achieved by repeating a shape, line or color.

perspective drawing   a method of drawing on a flat surface (which is two-dimensional) to give the illusion of depth, or the third dimension.

piers   heavy squarish columns that are the major supports for a dome or roof.

Plasticine   an oil-based clay, used for modeling. It usually stays workable and does not dry out.

Pop Art   a style of art that features the everyday, popular things around us. A drawing of a large Coke bottle might be considered Pop Art.

portrait   a piece of artwork featuring a person, several people or an animal. Portraits are usually facial, but can also be full figure.

positive space   the objects in a work of art, not the background or the space around them.

poster   a graphic design created for the purpose of promoting or selling a product or announcing an event.

Post-Impressionism   style of art that immediately followed the Impressionists in France. Cézanne was a leader of this style which stressed more substantial subjects and methods than those used by the Impressionists.

preliminary sketch   a planning sketch, usually on a small scale, to determine the basic arrangement of a design or larger work of art.

printmaking   any of several techniques for making multiple copies of a single image. Some examples are woodcuts, etchings, collagraphs and silk-screen prints.

product designer   artist who designs and gives style to manufactured products such as appliances, toys, automobiles, lighting, furniture.

proportion   a comparative size relationship between several objects or between the parts of a single object or person. In drawing, for example, get the correct relationship between the sizes of the head and body.

radial balance   a design based on a circle with the features radiating from a central point.

Realism   a style of art that realistically shows actual places, people or objects. It stresses actual colors, textures, shadows and arrangements.

relief   the raised parts of a surface that are often noticeable by the feeling of texture.

relief sculpture   a three-dimensional sculpture designed to be viewed from one side. Usually it is placed on a wall.

Renaissance   a period of time (1400–1600) following the Middle Ages. It emphasized human beings, their environment, science and philosophy. A renewal of Greek and Roman thinking regarding art and humanity.

resist   drawing and painting technique that relies on the fact that wax or oil will resist water, causing it to move to clean areas.

rhythm   a principle of design that indicates a type of movement in an artwork or design, often by repeated shapes or colors.

Rococo   a style of art (1700s) following the Baroque. It featured decorative and elegant themes and style.

Roman arch   same as the true arch. An arch with a rounded top (half circle). It was first used extensively by the ancient Romans.

Roman Art   the architecture and art of the ancient Roman peoples.

Romanesque Art   the style of architecture and art of western and southern Europe in the eleventh and twelfth centuries; usually related to churches and religious art.

Romanticism   a style of painting (mid–nineteenth century) that featured adventure, action, imagination and an interest in foreign happenings and people.

rubbing   a technique that transfers surface texture to paper by placing the paper over the textured surface and rubbing the top of the paper with a crayon or pencil.

sculpture   a carving, construction, casting or modelled form done in three-dimensions, height, width and depth.

seascape   a drawing or painting that features part of the sea as subject matter, often a coastal environment.

serigraph   a print (same as a silk-screen print) that is made by forcing ink through a stencil and silk-screen to paper below.

set-up   a group of objects arranged to be drawn or painted. A still life grouping.

shading   using two-dimensional medium to create darkened areas (shadows) that produce a feeling of space and depth.

shape   an element of design described as two-dimensional and enclosing area. Shape can be divided into two basic classes: geometric (square, triangle, circle) and organic (irregular in outline).

shaped canvas   a twentieth-century painting technique in which the canvas ground (surface) is not flat, but has objects placed behind it to form a relief surface.

silk-screen print   same as serigraph.

sketch   a quick drawing that catches the immediate feeling of action or the impression of a place. Probably not a completed drawing, but may be a reference for later work.

space   an element of design that indicates areas in a drawing (positive and negative) and/or the feeling of depth in a two-dimensional work of art.

stained glass   the brightly colored pieces of glass used in windows and held together with strips of lead. First used in churches of the Romanesque times.

still life   an arrangement of inanimate objects to draw or paint. Also, a drawing or painting of a set-up.

stitchery   a textile technique in which the design is created on cloth with a variety of stitches.

street painting   mural paintings done by nonprofessional artists. Usually they are painted on store sides, freeway retaining walls or fences.

subject matter   the things about which the artist is communicating in a work of art.

subtle   the delicate appearance or gradual change contained in a work of art. Hardly noticeable, unless a person looks carefully.

Super Realism   a style of drawing and painting in the late twentieth century that emphasizes photographic realism. The objects may be greatly enlarged, yet keep their photographic appearance.

surface decorating   techniques for creating designs on the surface of clay objects.

Surrealism   a style of twentieth-century painting in which the artists link normally unrelated objects and situations. Often the scenes are dreamlike or set in unnatural surroundings.

symmetrical balance   a design with one half that is a mirror-image of the other half.

technique   any method of working with materials.

textiles   objects made with cloth or fibrous materials.

texture   an element of design that refers to the surface quality (rough, smooth, soft). Texture can be actual or implied.

three-dimensional materials   materials such as clay, plaster, wood, metal and yarns, used to create forms that have three dimensions.

three dimensions   height, width and depth. A vase has three dimensions; a picture of it has only two dimensions.

tie-bleach   similar to tye-dye. Tied cloth is immersed in bleach to remove exposed color.

tie-dye   a textile design technique in which the design is created by tying the cloth and immersing in dye.

traditional art   any style of art that treats the subject matter in a natural (rather realistic) way. A style similar to those used for many years.

transparent   the quality of an object or paper that allows objects to be seen clearly through it, such as cellophane.

true arch   same as Roman arch. An arch with a semicircular top.

two-dimensional materials   materials such as paints, chalks and inks that are generally used on flat surfaces.

unity   a principle of design that relates to the sense of oneness or wholeness in a work of art.

urban areas   parts of cities where trade and commerce, business and industry are conducted. Educational, recreational and cultural interests are woven into the lifestyle of the people living in urban areas.

value   an element of design that relates to the lightness and darkness of a color or shade.

vertical   upright and parallel to the sides of the paper or canvas. A standing tree is vertical.

visual environment   everything that surrounds you, usually divided into two groupings: the natural environment (trees, flowers, water, sky, rocks) and the manufactured or built environment (buildings, roads, bridges, automobiles).

warp   fibrous material (yarn) interlaced vertically with the horizontal weft in a weaving.

wash   ink or watercolor paint that is diluted with water to make it lighter in value and more transparent.

weaving   the interlacing of threads and other materials to create a textile design as an integral part of cloth.

wedging   a technique in which clay is cut and slammed together several times to remove air bubbles and to produce an even texture in the clay.

wedging board   equipment used to wedge clay.

weft   horizontal threads in a weaving.

wet clay   clay that can be fired in a kiln when it is dry.

woodcut   a type of relief print, pulled from a block of wood whose surface has been cut and gouged to create the design.

Index

Acknowledgments

Gathering the visual material to produce this book has been an effort that involves many people. We would like to express our thanks to the following art teachers who provided visual materials for the book: Gerald Citrin, Laura deWyngaert, Joseph Gatto, Gene Gill, Helen Liutjens, Michael O'Brien, Al Porter, Jack Selleck, Roland Sylwester, and Norma Wrege.

The following artists were extremely generous in sending photos of their work to be included in the book, and we thank them for their help: Carole Barnes, Romare Bearden, Steven Bieck, John Biggers, Colleen Browning, Elena Canavier, Lynn Cartwright, Judy Chicago, Christo, Chuck Close, Nanci B. Clossen, Robert Cottingham, Gil DiCicco, Elaine de Kooning, Willem de Kooning, Joel Edwards, Janet Fish, Audrey Flack, Joseph Gatto, John Goodheart, Charles Gregson, Eric Gronborg, Jason Hailey, Roger Hagen, Frederick Hammersley, Duane Hanson, Rick Herold, Robert Irwin, George James, Dong Kingman, Jerome Kirk, Kathlene Knipple, Vivian Sauber Koos, Lee Krasner, Harrison McIntosh, Sam Maloof, Reinhold Marxhausen, Glen Michaels, Otto Natzler, LeRoy Nieman, Carla Pagliaro, Bob Peck, Kevin Red Star, Clare Romano, Teri Sandison, Arthur Secunda, Eilene Senner, Frank Stella, Roland Sylwester, Kent Ullberg, Veloy Vigil, Bert Wasserman, Charles White, Richard Wiegmann, Tyrus Wong and Robert E. Wood.

Our sincere appreciation to the staffs of the following galleries for allowing us to reproduce the work of artists they represent: Kennedy Galleries, New York; Leo Castelli Galleries, New York; Louis Meisel Gallery, New York; Louis Newman Galleries, Beverly Hills; Orlando Gallery, Sherman Oaks, California; Pace Gallery, New York; Robert Miller Gallery, New York; and the Treasure State Gallery, Great Falls, Montana.

We are grateful to personnel of the following museums which granted permission to use works contained in their collections: Albertina Museum, Vienna; Albright-Knox Art Gallery, Buffalo; Archaeological Museum, Candia, Crete; Art Institute of Chicago; Dallas Museum of Fine Arts; Franklin J. Murphy Sculpture Garden, UCLA; Frick Collection, New York; Jefferson Medical College, Philadelphia; Los Angeles County Museum of Art; The Louvre, Paris; Metropolitan Museum of Art, New York; Museum of Fine Arts, Boston; Museum of Modern Art, New York; National Gallery, Washington, D.C.; Norton Simon Inc. Foundation, Los Angeles; Norton Simon Museum, Pasadena; Philadelphia Museum of Art; The Prado, Madrid; St. Peters, The Vatican; San Francisco Museum of Modern Art; Tate Gallery, London; Whitney Museum of American Art, New York.

The following firms and governmental agencies were extremely cooperative in supplying visual materials for this book: Adler, Schwartz Graphics, Inc., Baltimore;, American Crafts Council, New York; American Yearbook Company, Visalia, California; Brown and Craig, Inc.; Carlos Diniz and Assoc.; Embassy of Turkey; Ford Motor Co.; General Electric Corp.; Harrison and Abramovitz; Houston Chamber of Commerce, Texas; IBM; Italian Cultural Institute; Johnson/Burgee, Architects; Marcel Breuer Associates; Meyers and D'Aleo, Inc.; Saul Bass and Associates; Scan, Baltimore; St. Regis Paper Co.; Spectralegends, Norfolk; Steve Chase and Associates, Palm Springs; R. Thomas and Associates, Utah Travel Council, WJXT, Jacksonville; Worcester Craft Center, Massachusetts.

To the hundreds of art teachers from across the country who encouraged us through their words and their use of the first edition of this text, your constant good will encouraged us to produce this second edition. Thank you.

Photo Credits

Teachers from many schools were helpful in supplying photos of student work for this book. Students are constantly producing work that is excellent in quality and exciting in concept. The pieces reproduced in this text are used because they help expand ideas presented in the text.

We are indebted to students from the following schools. The numbers indicate the pages on which the work is found. Auburn Junior H.S., Maine: 234. Baltimore Public Schools: 35, 53, 218, 219, 220, 221, 222, 223, 224, 225, 227, 228, 230, 231, 235, 241, 244, 245, 246, 247. Bancroft Junior H.S.: 153, 165, Carver Junior H.S.: 105, 134, Emerson Junior H.S.: 1, 65, 113, 115, 133, 139, 146, 170, 175, 177, 186, 230, LeConte Junior H.S.: 180, Lutheran Junior H.S.: 4, 50, 99, 104, 106, 107, 109, 110, 111, 114, 116, 117, 118, 119, 122, 128, 129, 133, 135, 138, 145, 147, 152, 155, 156, 157, 158, 160, 161, 165, 172, 174, 179, 182, 183, 204, 205, 210, 211, 230, Nightingale Junior H.S.: 119, Paul Revere Junior H.S.: 130 (all Los Angeles, California). Fairmont Middle School, Minnesota: 230. Gardena H.S., California: 64, 142. Junior High North, Connersville, Indiana: 230. Kent City Junior H.S., Minnesota, 230. Reseda H.S., California: 3, 140. Seoul American Junior and Senior H.S., Seoul, Korea: 51, 52, 105, 106, 110, 112, 113, 120, 131, 137, 140, 161, 204, 208, 210, 211, 216, 238, 242, 243. Sleeping Giant Junior H.S., Hamden, Connecticut: 22. Southgate Junior H.S., California: 143. Thorne Junior H.S., Port Monmouth, New Jersey: 136, 173. Art Center College of Design, Pasadena: 28.

The visual images in this book are a constant reminder of the fine work done by America's photographers. Their work is greatly appreciated by the authors, and we would like to thank them here: Peter Aaron, 39. Frank Armstrong, 16. G. Crossboard: 147. Esto Photographics: 39. Peter Faulkner: 44. Joseph Gatto: 46, 166, 173, 203, 213, 216, 217. Jason Hailey: 26. Alice Hall: 34. Thomas Jewell: 16. Larry Jones: 21. Beverly Klemola: 14. Gretta Moore: 42. Joseph Molitor: 12, 39. Gail Reynolds Natzler: 53, 57, 217, 232. Peter Palmquist: 213. Rick Paulson: 45. Al Porter: 33, 107, 112, 132. Teri Sandison: 203. Shunk-Kender: 11. Linda Umgelter: 37.